PASS YOUR
YACHTMASTER

Fifth Edition

PASS YOUR YACHTMASTER

Fifth Edition

DAVID FAIRHALL • MIKE PEYTON

ADLARD COLES NAUTICAL
London

Published by Adlard Coles Nautical
an imprint of Bloomsbury Publishing Plc
50 Bedford Square, London WC1B 3DP
www.adlardcoles.com

Copyright © David Fairhall and Mike Peyton 1982, 1989, 2002, 2006, 2011

First edition published by Nautical Books 1982
Reprinted (with corrections) 1983
Reprinted 1986
Second edition 1989
Third edition published by Adlard Coles Nautical 2002
Fourth edition 2006
Fifth edition 2011

ISBN: 978-1-4081-5284-3
Epub ISBN: 978-1-4081-5627-8
E-PDF ISBN: 978-1-4081-4628-6

A CIP catalogue record for this book is available from the British Library.

This book is produced using paper that is made from wood grown in
managed, sustainable forests. It is natural, renewable and recyclable.
The logging and manufacturing processes conform to the
environmental regulations of the country of origin.

Typeset in Frutiger 9/11pt by Margaret Brain
Pantone 284C
Printed and bound in China by RR Donnelly, South China

Note: While all reasonable care has been taken in the publication
of this book, the publisher takes no responsibility for the use of the methods
or products described in the book.

Acknowledgements
The tidal extracts are used with kind permission of The Controller HMSO
and the Hydrographer of the Navy.

Yachtmaster™ is a trademark of the Royal Yachting Association
registered in the United Kingdom and selected marketing territories.
For information on RYA qualifications and RYA approved training courses for both
power and sail please visit the website: www.rya.org.uk/courses
or telephone: 0845 345 0384 (from overseas telephone +44 23 8060 4100),
or write to: RYA Training, RYA House, Ensign Way, Hamble, Southampton SO31 4YA

Contents

'We're dragging all right, and fast...'

Introduction

The Yachtmaster Offshore course is part of an extensive voluntary training scheme run by the Royal Yachting Association 'to encourage high standards of seamanship and navigation among yachtsmen and women' and avoid unnecessary regulation. Each year thousands of yachtsmen and women attend evening classes as a preparation for the coveted Yachtmaster qualification – or perhaps just as a change from learning French. This book is unashamedly a 'crammer' for that course – updated in this new edition to incorporate the latest developments in electronic navigation and safety procedures.

The RYA prefers not to talk about its shorebased courses as an examination process – it merely awards 'certificates of satisfactory completion'. But whatever you call the exercises and assessment papers, they strike most students as being exams in a format they may not have faced since leaving school. Indeed, some of the exercises have to be taken under invigilation and require detailed knowledge that needs 'swotting up' beforehand. And that is where this book comes in.

We have tried to help by looking for the logic as well as the facts, and eliminating unnecessary information to concentrate on the essentials of the RYA syllabus. In each of the main sections – **navigation, weather, safety and seagoing practice** – we have tried to do four things:

- Provide all the essential information.
- Organise it in a digestible form that makes learning and revision easier – in fact, the book is small enough to slip in your pocket to skim through in the lunch hour, on the train home, or just before going into the exam.
- Advise on exam tactics.
- Set all this in a practical seagoing perspective.

No single textbook is a substitute for the extensive background reading needed, let alone for the instruction itself. But we can provide a skeleton, waiting to be fleshed out by teaching, reading and practical experience, because ultimately there is also no substitute for seatime.

'And after you've got the matches, just ask casually what lighthouse it is.'

The RYA training scheme operates at five main levels – Competent Crew, Day Skipper/Watch Leader, Coastal Skipper, Yachtmaster Offshore, and Yachtmaster Ocean. Courses cover all of these (plus motor cruising helmsmanship, diesel engine maintenance, radar and survival) with practical exams for the last three.

The shorebased course we are concerned with here is a combined one, for **Coastal Skipper/Yachtmaster Offshore** candidates. It involves a minimum of 40 hours teaching plus work at home. The syllabus is set out in RYA booklets, for sail and power. To obtain the final Offshore qualification, or 'certificate of competence', you must first log 50 days at sea, covering 2500 miles, including at least five 60-mile passages, and also hold a radio operator's certificate and a first aid certificate. The practical exam, for which you may need to provide the boat, lasts 8–12 hours, and aims to show that you can competently skipper a cruising yacht up to 150 miles offshore.

We hope this book gets you successfully under way.

To make things easier, we have used **bold** type and tinted panels to pick out key phrases and facts to help you with your revision.

The symbols at the bottom of each right hand page are to test your knowledge – the answers are overleaf.

Navigation

European navigators first acquired a primitive magnetic compass at least 800 years ago, possibly from China, where the invention was recorded even earlier. Nowadays, courtesy of the US Defense Department, we have navigational satellites to provide a Global Positioning System (GPS) accurate to within a few metres.

But neither of these great technological advances would be much use to us without a chart, to identify our destination and warn of obstacles along the way. Buoys and lighthouses confirming the changing position are also shown on the chart. And, independent of GPS, we also need to be able to measure speed and distance, and find the depth of water. So this section of the book deals with all these sources of navigational information, plus other related subjects covered by the Yachtmaster™ assessment papers.

The offshore racing yachtsman likes to know precisely where he is at all times. In contrast, those who are cruising can take things a bit easier, provided they anticipate the occasions when they really *do* need an accurate position: winding through sandbanks on a falling tide, for instance, or making landfall in bad visibility. In practice, therefore, navigational techniques range all the way from the crumpled-chart-on-the-cockpit-seat school, right through to the pedantic naval style that expects to have a course plotted from the harbour berth to the pierheads. The would-be Yachtmaster should remember he is still in the classroom preparing for an exam, and so take his cue from the instructor.

Charts

Like land maps, charts are the projection of a curved surface on to a flat sheet of paper. **The common projection is Mercator's.** This spreads out the lines of longitude (measured in degrees east or west of the Greenwich meridian) so that they appear parallel instead of converging at the North Pole, as they do on a globe. But to preserve the shape of the coastline, lines of latitude (measured in degrees from the Equator) also have to spread out as you move north.

An important practical implication of this is that **distances should always be measured along the side of the chart**, where latitude is marked, roughly level with the yacht's position. One minute of latitude – a sixtieth of a degree – is a **nautical mile**, and it averages out (because the earth is not exactly spherical) at

'I've brought our position up to date, John. Give me a call when we sight land.'

6076 feet or 1852 metres. A **cable** is a tenth of a nautical mile, roughly 200 yards.

On Mercator charts a straight line, or **rhumb line**, is not the shortest distance between two real points. That would be a **great circle**, which appears on the chart as a curved line. In practice, this distortion rarely matters to yachtsmen. However, some charts do show lines of longitude converging as they would on a globe, using a **Gnomonic projection**, so that the shortest distance across an ocean can conveniently be drawn as a straight line.

UK charts are drawn from underwater surveys commissioned by the UK Hydrographic Office (UKHO), supplemented by information from similar organisations abroad, and marketed as *Admiralty* charts. This comprehensive series sets the standard. However, these paper charts are primarily designed for use on the full-sized chart table of a large merchant vessel or warship, so the UKHO has recently produced *Small Craft Folios* (but only for UK waters) to match those published specifically for yachtsmen by Imray and Stanfords. Individual sailors will have their own preferences regarding these yachting charts, but they are all suitable for use in a damp cockpit and stuffed into a transparent plastic cover, not just in a sheltered chartroom. The charts also provide lots of supplementary information, selected and presented from the perspective of a small boat rather than a supertanker. Harbour plans and miniature tidal stream charts are particularly useful.

One thing you need to know about any chart is whether it is up to date. Minor changes occur frequently and are often important. It can be extremely disconcerting when a buoy turns up in the 'wrong' position, in a different shape, or simply disappears.

North cardinal buoy

On Admiralty charts, the date of the edition is shown in the margin, plus a reference to the weekly *Notices to Mariners* where relevant corrections are published. Imray give the edition date and attach a list of corrections. Stanfords give the edition and the date to which each chart is corrected. All three publishers can supply further corrections by post and on their respective websites.

Electronic charts

These come in two forms – **raster** and **vector** – displayed on the screen of a dedicated chart plotter or, if you prefer, a laptop computer. Raster charts are simply photographed from the original with a digital camera, losing definition if the scale is enlarged too far. Vector charts are produced from scratch in computerised form, a more complex but flexible method enabling information to be edited to suit the scale. (Ships using the vector system can dispense with paper charts, but this is certainly not recommended for yachts.) The big advantage of electronic charts is that GPS position information, and even radar, can be integrated with the display, although you will practise your basic navigation on a paper chart.

Units of depth on charts

The traditional **unit of depth** at sea is the fathom – 6 feet – and some charts, particularly in the USA, still use fathoms. However, nearly all European charts now mark minimum depths in metres and tenths of a metre, so for the purpose of the Yachtmaster course you need only think metric. Where the little numbers scattered across the chart are underlined, this shows the **drying height** above low water.

Symbols

There are thousands of other **symbols and abbreviations**, listed as *Admiralty Chart No 5011* (which is actually a booklet), and many are self-explanatory – like the little drawings of buoys with their various topmarks. Others, such as the symbol for lava flowing down the side of a volcano, can safely be ignored. In any case, this is an area where your instructor will probably allow you to consult sources of reference, unlike when you are sitting the assessment papers on collision regulations, meteorology and chartwork, which must be done under exam conditions.

Many students will be content simply to learn the common symbols as they crop up, but if you do want to do a bit of swotting, some categories are obviously of more importance than others. Ways of marking wrecks and dangerous rocks are one such example, as are the descriptions of light characteristics.

Some commonly used symbols and abbreviations

Wk	wreck	
	wreck showing at chart datum (very low water)	
	wreck considered dangerous	
	wreck over which depth, as shown, has been sounded	
	wreck not considered dangerous	
	rock awash at chart datum (very low water)	
	underwater rock, depth unknown	
	overfalls or tide rip	
	underwater cable	
S	sand	
M	mud	
Sn	shingle	
Sh	shells	

Light symbol abbreviations

R	red
G	green
W	white
F	fixed (steady light)
Fl	single flashing
L Fl	long flashing (at least 2 seconds)
Fl(3)	group flashing (groups of 3)
Q	continuous quick flashing
Q(3)	groups of 3 quick flashes
IQ	interrupted quick flashing
VQ	continuous very quick flashing
VQ(3)	groups of 3 very quick flashes
IVQ	interrupted very quick flashing
Oc	occulting (only short periods of darkness)
Iso	isophase (equal periods of darkness and light)

Recommended anchorage

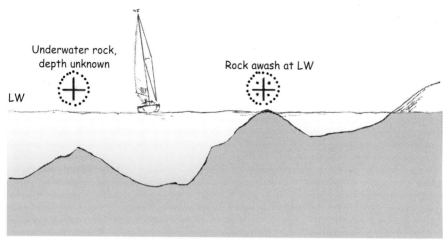

Chart symbols.

Lighthouses

On a metric chart, a small lighthouse might be annotated Fl(2)WRG 10s 14m 7–5M. This means that its light flashes twice every ten seconds; it has three fixed sectors showing white, red and green; it stands 14 metres above high water on a spring tide; and the **luminous range** of its multi-coloured light is from 5 to 7 nautical miles. (Note the possible confusion between lower case m for metres and upper case M for miles.) The luminous range is the distance from which the lighthouse can be seen in clear visibility – which is also the **nominal range** when 'clear' visibility is defined as 10 miles. It's important to realise that the **geographical range** may be different again – that is, the distance at which a powerful light shows above the horizon if your eye level is 15 feet above the water (as it might have been on an old sailing ship). The 'loom' of a powerful lighthouse from seaward is often visible before the actual light rises above the horizon – a fascinating phenomenon that can help fix your position, as we shall see later.

The IALA buoyage system

Navigational buoys are distinguished by shape, colour and the light they show. Their arrangement follows two main principles – lateral and cardinal.

The lateral and cardinal systems

In a **lateral** system (traditionally used in British waters) buoys are laid to port and starboard of the navigable water according to what is known as the conventional direction of buoyage – which runs from SW to NE round the British Isles and then into the various estuaries and rivers. This method lends itself to marking a clearly defined channel, especially in an estuary, like the Thames, where the conventional direction is also the direction of the flood tide and the way into port.

In a **cardinal** system (formerly associated with Continental waters) buoys are distinguished according to the cardinal points of the compass – N, E, S and W – and placed in that direction from the point of interest or danger they mark. This method is particularly suitable for marking, say, the edges of an offshore sandbank or a coastal reef, although it can also mark the features of a channel.

'There's the East Knock.'

The **IALA System A** used in Europe (IALA is the International Association of Lighthouse Authorities) combines both lateral and cardinal principles – port and starboard marks for channels, and mainly cardinal ones for other features.

Lateral marks on the port side of a channel are flat-topped can or pillar buoys, while those to starboard are conical or pointed. They are coloured red to port and green to starboard, as are the lights they show – which match the colours of a ship's navigational sidelights. At night, therefore, it is the colour of a buoy's light that conveys its basic message, rather than the light's rhythm, which varies merely to distinguish individual buoys.

Observed position

Cardinal marks adopt the opposite approach, using the rhythm of the light – which is always white – as well as the buoy's shape and colour to convey its message. These are tall black and yellow buoys with a distinguishing topmark formed by two black cones. We think of the North Pole as the 'top' of the world, so the two cones of a north cardinal topmark both point upwards and those on a south cardinal buoy point downwards (like the traditional gale warning cones). To help remember the west and east topmarks, with their two cones pointing in opposite directions, the shapes they form are often compared to a **W**ineglass and an **E**gg respectively. The black and yellow bands on the buoy's structure (see diagram in centre colour section) have a similar logic to them, though seaweed and rust can sometimes confuse the pattern.

Light characteristics

As for the **light characteristics**, notice that they are arranged rather like a clock face – continuous single flashing for north, a group of three flashes for east at 'three o'clock', six for south (plus a distinguishing long flash) and nine for west. The shorter flashes can be either 'quick' (about once a second) or 'very quick' (twice a second).

An **occulting** light (not to be confused with the occluded front in meteorology) stays lit most of the time, with only short periods of darkness – in other words, the opposite of a flashing light. The description **isophase** (compare with **isobar**) means that the periods of light and dark are equal. It is important to note that these last two characteristics are both associated with safety in the IALA buoyage system. The opposite message comes from the double white flash of a black and red buoy marking an isolated danger, and carrying two black spheres as a topmark.

Three other points to remember about buoys

- They make excellent tidal stream indicators.
- They must have a fair scope of mooring chain to cope with the tidal range, so their position can never be absolutely precise.
- If they are laid to mark a deep-dredged channel for large ships, it is probably sensible for a small, slow-moving yacht to stay outside – in other words, on the 'wrong' side of them.

'No wonder you couldn't find them darling, they're all here!'

The compass

There are 32 points on a full compass rose, each measuring 11¼° of the circle. But on a modern yacht steering compass, only four (or maybe eight) points are usually marked – N, NE, E, SE, and so on. The primary marking is in degrees from 0° to 360°, probably at intervals of 5°. This is about the smallest margin of error you can hope for in steering a sailing boat, although on the chart you lay a course to the nearest degree.

The course is held by keeping some sort of fore-and-aft 'lubber line' against the required mark on the compass card, or by setting an adjustable steering grid on top of the compass card to the chosen course and then lining up the compass needle – and hence the boat – with it. A grid design with luminous paint might just be usable at night, but most compasses are lit either by a small conventional bulb or by a beta light.

The traditional compass in its binnacle is read from above, but some are designed for mounting in a vertical bulkhead or on top of a coachroof, and can be read from the side. The important thing is to position the compass as far as possible from the magnetic interference of the ferrous metals that are always present in a boat's engine, often in the keel, and in various fittings round the cockpit. You should also avoid putting the compass near electrical equipment such as radios and echo sounders.

Major light

An **electronic** or **fluxgate** compass will also sense and indicate north. Because it can be linked to other electronic equipment, it has useful specialised applications such as providing heading information for an autopilot or stabilising a radar display.

Deviation

However carefully a compass needle is sited, though, it is almost bound to show some **deviation** from the Earth's magnetic pole, if only by a few degrees east or west. A large deviation can be roughly checked by comparison with a hand bearing compass held well away from possible interference. This will vary with the boat's heading, so accurate navigation – and the syllabus chartwork – require the use of a **deviation card** showing the error in degrees E or W for every couple of compass points or, better still, a curve on which the error associated with any given course can be interpolated. In practice, even a substantial error may not matter on a short coastal trip, although it certainly will on a long sea crossing.

Preparing an accurate card for your own boat is a complicated procedure that involves turning her slowly through successive headings while checking the steering compass against the known bearing of a distant object – or, alternatively, building up a card as opportunities arise during the season. Fortunately, the Yachtmaster course notes provide a standard deviation table.

Variation

Compass work also involves a more fundamental allowance for the **variation** between the direction of the magnetic pole and true north as shown by the lines of longitude. The compass rose printed on a chart is usually two roses, one inside the other, providing both true bearings or courses, and magnetic ones. In our part of the world, a compass needle points slightly west of true north. In the southern North Sea, for example, the present variation is about 3° W and slowly decreasing.

It is possible to navigate entirely with magnetic bearings and courses, using the inner ring of the compass rose. The raw data coming from the yacht's steering and hand bearing compasses is, after all, in this form. But the chart grid is laid out on a true basis, and much of the other information you will need – for example, tidal streams – is presented in the same way. So whichever way you work, the problem of **converting from magnetic bearings to true and back again** is going to arise – and in the navigational classroom it occurs only too often! One of the first things to acquire, therefore, is some foolproof way of remembering and checking this procedure.

Look at a compass rose, and you will see that with 3° westerly variation, a magnetic bearing is always that many degrees more than its true equivalent.

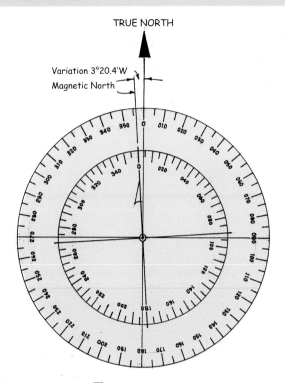

TRUE NORTH

Variation 3°20.4'W

Magnetic North

The compass rose.

True north lines up with 3° magnetic (0T=3M), true south lines up with 183° magnetic (180T=183M), and so on. The same would apply if the compass difference was a combination of westerly variation and westerly deviation – say 3° variation and 2° deviation – a total of 5° W to be subtracted from the compass bearing (which in this case, because of its deviation error, is not the same as the magnetic bearing) to make it true. True south would now line up with 185° on the compass (180T=185C).

On the other hand, if the compass error is to the east – say an easterly deviation of 5° offset by 3° westerly variation, leaving a net error of 2° E – then the opposite rule will apply. The 2° E must be added to convert a compass reading to true (or, of course, subtracted to convert the other way).

At sea, this particular calculation is usually simpler than it probably looks here. For any given area, variation can be treated as constant, and the more time compass deviation has to work its mischief, the more time you have to get it right. In the classroom, people use various tricks and mnemonics to help them, such as:

Port hand buoy

> Variation West, Compass Best,
> ADDECT (ADD Easterly Compass to True).

Your instructor will no doubt suggest others. But unless you prefer to work it out from first principles each time, find something that suits you and stick to it.

The log

A log can measure both speed through the water and the distance covered, because of course one determines the other. But it is the latter information that the navigator ultimately needs in order to calculate his position and to check when he should start looking for a landfall.

As the name suggests, this piece of navigational equipment started as a wooden log thrown over the stern on a line, to see how fast the knots marking the line ran out (hence also the nautical term **knots**, meaning nautical miles per hour). Nowadays, the log exists in many forms – **towed (mechanical or electrical), retractable hull-mounted, doppler or ultrasonic**. As with most things, each type has its pros and cons.

The traditional patent log consisted of a counter mounted on the stern rail, driven mechanically by a spinner at the end of a line (no battery to go flat, but the rotating line was lethal for exhausted migrating birds). The electronic equivalent (the spinner generates a small, measurable current) is highly accurate, but it still has to be streamed and recovered.

The usual modern alternative generates the electrical current by a small retractable propeller or paddle wheel mounted through the hull. Once inserted, it is always ready for use, but is easily fouled by weed and mud.

Other logs use the doppler principle – highly accurate, with no holes in the hull or moving parts, but they need careful positioning – or an ultrasonic sensor.

Depth sounding

The traditional method of sounding shallow depths at sea is the **lead line** – a line marked in fathoms with strips of leather and bunting, attached to a lump of lead hollowed out at the bottom and 'armed' with sticky tallow. For routine depth measurement, it has long since been replaced by the echo sounder. Yet the lead still has a useful place on board a yacht: as a back-up; to 'feel' the uneven bottom round an anchorage; to calibrate your echo sounder; or even to test those chart symbols describing the seabed as mud (M), shells (Sh) or shingle (Sn).

fS.M.Sh

An **echo sounder** works by measuring the time it takes for an ultrasonic pulse emitted by a hull-mounted transducer to be reflected back from the seabed. There are four main types of display – **digital, rotating LED (light emitting diode), dial**, and **trace** – each with its own advantages. Simplest is the digital display in metres or feet. The dial's moving pointer gives a clear sense of changes in depth, while the 'fishfinder' trace shows the seabed contours. The classic in this field is the rotating LED, which clearly shows movement and is easily seen at night, though it does require periodic adjustment to eliminate a secondary echo.

The echo sounder is an invaluable aid to pilotage and navigation, especially when fitted with a **depth alarm**. The alarm can be set to warn of dangerously shallow water, to signal the alignment of a deep trough in the seabed, or help the navigator follow a depth contour in bad visibility. The display can be calibrated either simply to show the depth or adjusted – particularly for shallow waters – to indicate the depth under a particular boat's keel.

GPS

The **Global Positioning System (GPS)** provides a constant read-out of a yacht's position – expressed in **latitude and longitude** – to an accuracy of a few metres.

This navigational miracle is worked by analysing coded signals from a 'birdcage' of US military satellites orbiting the earth. Given a series of such positions, even the most modest GPS computer can instantly work out the yacht's course and speed over the ground, calculate the range and bearing of any specified **waypoint (WPT)** on the chart (also defined by its Lat and Long), and subsequently the amount by which the yacht deviates from the direct track towards it – the **cross track error (XTE)**.

Yet the installation that provides all this is less complex (eg in the siting of the aerial) than for a VHF radio. Handheld GPS sets resemble mobile phones.

There are two secondary systems which make GPS even more accurate. The **Differential Global Positioning System (DGPS)** checks the satellite signals against known positions on the ground, but requires additional dedicated equipment. The **Satellite Differential Ground Position System (SDGPS)** also uses ground stations to monitor GPS signals, but transmits corrections by satellite through the same equipment – if suitably modified – which handles the basic information.

Apart from constantly updating your position, the key to the GPS's usefulness is that navigational complications such as tidal streams, leeway, or even tacking to windward do not bother it. It will display your **speed over the ground (SOG)**, the important information you probably want, not the speed through the water indicated by the boat's log. As you beat towards a GPS mark, up comes the net **velocity made good (VMG)**.

Fine sand with mud and shells

'One must admit, going from waypoint to waypoint on autohelm takes
the excitement out of sailing.'

What is more, this extraordinary computational capacity is increasingly integrated with electronic charts to create a **chart plotter**, displaying the yacht's
position as it moves across the chart – in effect a complete navigational system
(See 'Electronic navigation').

Radar

Radar is a valuable source of general navigational information – such as the
position lines we shall deal with later – as well as a specific means of collision
avoidance. On small sailing yachts it is hard to get a satisfactory installation,
either on the mast or the stern. On motor yachts, however, with no sails to get
in the way, it really comes into its own, and can be integrated with other
features of the electronic chart plotter. When reading a raw radar display
remember that the movement you see is **relative** to your own boat's heading
and speed. Forgetting this has led to so-called 'radar-assisted collisions'.

$\longrightarrow$

Tides

Tides are caused by the gravitational pull of the moon and, to a lesser extent, the sun. The orbiting moon produces two high tides every day or, to be a little more precise, in a period of about 24 hours 50 minutes – which is why the time of high water is about 50 minutes later each day.

When the moon is full, or new, the sun's gravitational pull is exerted in the same direction. The movement of water is greater, tidal streams run faster, and the tide rises higher (and falls lower) than at other times. Such conditions are known as **spring tides**. They occur every two weeks, in keeping with the phases of the moon; and at any given place on the coast, high water springs will be at roughly the same time of day.

But in alternate weeks, when the sun is pulling at right angles to the moon, the tidal range from high to low water is smaller. These are **neap tides** – less useful if you are trying to float your boat out of a mud berth, but also less of a hazard when crossing a shallow bar at low water. Spring tides, incidentally, are especially high and low during the spring and in the autumn.

Depths shown on a chart are measured from a level known as the **chart datum** – either the mean level of low water spring tides (**MLWS**) or, more commonly, the level of the lowest astronomically predictable tide (**LAT**). The height of a tide is also measured from the chart datum, as is the height of a drying sandbank. But note that the height of a lighthouse is measured from mean high water springs (**MHWS**) – a point easily forgotten when facing an exam question about the distance at which the light is visible.

At the centre of this oscillating pattern of rising and falling tides is a **mean level (ML)**.

Tide tables

The primary source of tidal predictions is the *Admiralty Tide Tables*. Volume 1 of this covers British waters, although tide tables are also available in many local publications and in **nautical almanacs** produced for yachtsmen.

Reeds Nautical Almanac, for instance, provides comprehensive tidal data for British and Continental waters, plus information on a vast range of other subjects – navigation (including passage planning, waypoints, tidal streams, pilotage and harbour charts), radio aids, weather forecasting, collision regulations, safety procedures and first aid. The almanac makes a plausible claim to contain all the nautical information needed to navigate British and European waters from Denmark to Gibraltar. At sea, therefore, such a publication is invaluable. In the classroom, too, it is a reasonable answer to give for almost any question about sources of information.

Opening the Admiralty **tide tables** at the pages dealing with the 'standard port' of Dover, you will find the times and heights of high and low water for

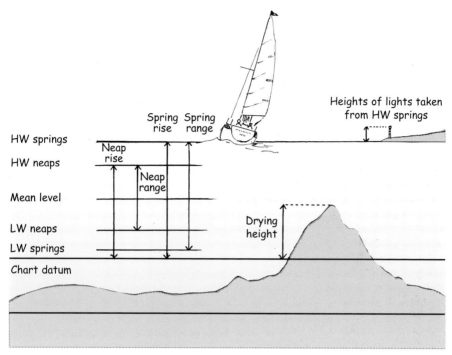

Definitions of the various tidal levels.

each day of the year (times in Universal Time, heights in metres). Associated with the table is a steeply humped **tidal curve** – or, to be more precise, two curves superimposed: a solid line for springs and a dashed line for neaps.

Tidal curves

These curves (now also available as laptop software) are the basis of the Admiralty method of tide calculation you will use for Yachtmaster exams. Note that their height is not marked directly in metres, but in proportional factors ranging from zero to 1.0 (at high tide), because the 'shape' of the tide is determined separately from its height. A horizontal scale across the base of the curves shows the time before and after high water. Until the curves are applied to the actual heights for a particular day, plotted on the left-hand side of the diagram, they merely show, for example, that on a rising spring tide at Dover, the water will rise by less than a tenth of its eventual range (a factor of less than 0.1) during the first hour (four hours before

'I thought you did all this at night school – working out tides, times, ranges . . .'

HW, not five, because this asymmetrical tide takes less time to rise than it does to fall). After five hours of a falling neap tide, the level will be down to about two-tenths of the range (a factor of 0.2), and so on.

Similar curves are shown for each of the **standard ports**. Some curves are quite symmetrical; others are sharply skewed. For ports in the Bristol Channel, where the tidal range is enormous, they are steeply peaked. On the east coast they are much flatter. For spring tides at Southampton the peak is double, indicating a second high water, because of the complex way that tides flow round the Isle of Wight and the surrounding area.

Rule of Twelfths

If you were to take all these individual curves and combine them in a single smooth symmetrical line – that is, the ideal pattern the tide would follow if there were nothing to distort its flow – that line could be expressed as a simple rule: the tide would rise or fall approximately one-twelfth of its range in the first hour after low or high water, two-twelfths in the second hour, three-twelfths in the third and fourth hours, two-twelfths again in the fifth hour, and one-twelfth in the sixth and final hour.

Isophase light (Iso) – equal light and dark periods

So if you find tidal calculations confusing (and, let's face it, many fine yachtsmen have no head for figures), you can fall back on this **Rule of Twelfths**: 1, 2, 3, 3, 2, 1.

On many occasions such a simple pattern will obviously be less accurate than the full calculation, especially where the tidal range is large or the shape asymmetrical. But then there are other sources of error in tidal predictions. A rise of only about 11 millibars in atmospheric pressure will lower the sea level by a tenth of a metre. A storm surge driving down the North Sea can raise tides by a

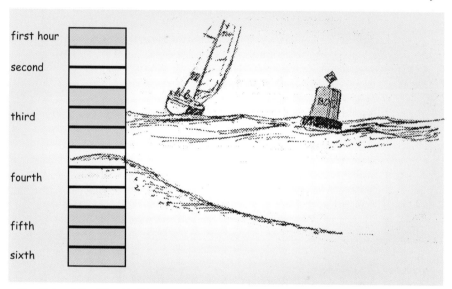

first hour

second

third

fourth

fifth

sixth

The Rule of Twelths. In this case the yacht is crossing the shoal two and a half hours after high water. In another hour, the shoal would be awash.

metre or more above their predicted level. Local effects are also powerful. At the head of an estuary, the incoming tide may arrive with great suddenness (the Severn bore is an extreme example) while the first of the ebb may rush away with surprising speed. Therefore a generous safety margin is always required, not least because near real rocks, or on a real bar, your boat will be bouncing up and down in the waves!

Back in the classroom, though, you will have to face an assessment paper that treats the tidal predictions as exact to a tenth of a metre, so you have to get the **Admiralty method** clear in your mind.

Making tidal calculations

To find the height of tide (at a standard port) **at a given time** between high and low water:

1 Calculate how many hours before or after HW your given time is, and mark it along the base of the curves (A).
2 From this starting point, draw a line vertically to meet the appropriate curve (springs or neaps) (A1).
3 Proceed horizontally to meet the sloping tide line showing the relevant range on the required day (A2).
4 Proceed vertically, up or down, to read off the height at your given time (A3).

To find the time at which the tide will reach a given height (at a standard port):

1 Starting from the required height on the horizontal height scale (B), draw a line vertically to meet the sloping tide line (B1).
2 Proceed horizontally to the appropriate curve (springs or neaps, rising or falling) (B2).
3 Proceed vertically down to read off the time before or after HW on the horizontal time scale (B3).

'According to my calculations, there's plenty of water.'

East cardinal buoy

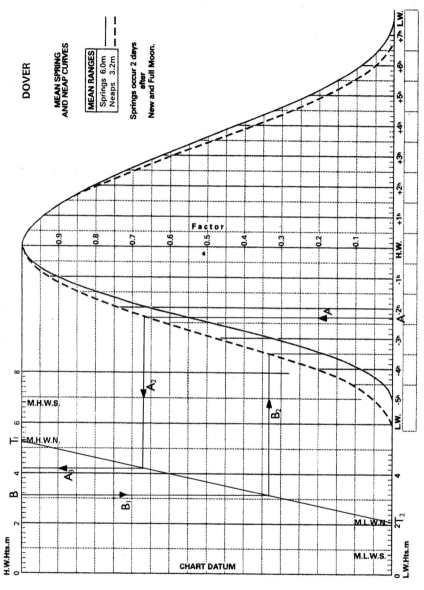

Extract from the Admiralty Tide Tables Vol 1 NP 201-02.

POOLE HARBOUR
MEAN SPRING AND NEAP CURVES
Springs occur 2 days after New and Full Moon.

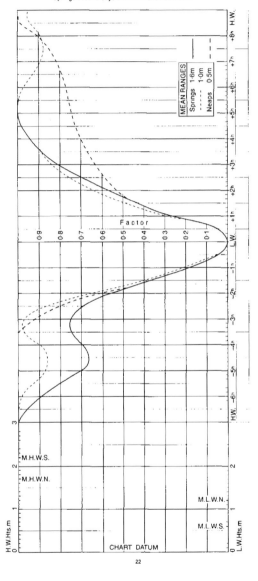

Extract from the Admiralty Tide Tables Vol 1 NP 201-02.

Safe water mark

There will obviously be many occasions when a calculation of the range (HW–LW) shows neither a spring nor a neap tide, but something in between. If the two curves for that port are significantly different, interpolate between them by eye, after checking the actual range against the ranges shown for springs and neaps.

Tidal curves for **secondary ports** are not normally available, so consult an almanac for time and height corrections to be applied to the appropriate standard-port curve. Bear in mind that the corrections vary according to the time and height of high or low water (whether it is springs or neaps), so there may be more interpolating to be done, graphically or otherwise.

For those sailing on the south coast of England, there is one other complication. Between Swanage and Selsey Bill, the shape of the tides is grossly distorted – so much so that, as we have seen, there may be a double high tide. Fortunately, low tide remains a single, clearly identified event, so tidal curves in this area are centred on LW. For some of these ports a third 'critical' curve is included because the shape of the spring and neap curves is so different.

Points to remember about tidal calculations

The practical seagoing message where tidal calculations are concerned is to match your method to the circumstances. Before crossing an exposed bar on a fast flowing ebb, it is obviously worth taking more trouble with your arithmetic, and allowing a bigger safety margin, than when easing into a muddy estuary on the flood.

Tidal streams

Information on tidal streams comes in two main forms: special little chartlets that may be made up into a **tidal stream atlas**, and **tidal diamonds**, which refer to a table of direction and speed.

On a set of chartlets (as found in an *Admiralty Tidal Stream Atlas*, in almanacs and on some charts) the streams at each hour before and after HW at a certain port are shown by a pattern of arrows marked with the rate in knots at springs and neaps. The arrows vary in thickness according to the strength of the tide. This presentation gives an excellent general impression.

Tidal diamonds are marked on the chart, and identified by letters. These refer to tables showing the **rate and direction** at each hour. (In case you come across the more traditional terms, the direction of a tide is sometimes referred to as the **set**, while the rate is the **drift**.) This presentation is convenient for plotting a course, because the direction of the tide can be read straight off as a true bearing (that is, the direction in which the tidal stream is flowing, not the direction from which it has come, as with winds).

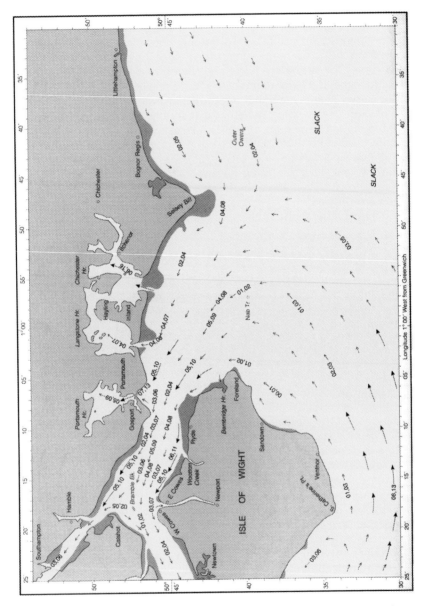

Extract from the Admiralty Tidal Stream Atlas for the Solent: one hour before high water Portsmouth.

Wreck visible at low water

Points to remember about tidal streams

- They run stronger in deep water.
- They tend to set into bays, and in the lee of a headland may even eddy in the reverse direction.
- They can be accelerated into tide rips or races where they have to force their way past headlands like Portland and the Lizard, or squeeze through a bottleneck like the notorious Pentland Firth. On a spring ebb, even the sandy river bars of the east coast can produce standing waves that will fill a small yacht's cockpit. A big race produces alarming, unpredictable waves even in calm weather and, if it is blowing, they should definitely be avoided – unless, as sometimes happens, there is a calm eddying patch close inshore through which you can slip.

Other basic sources of information

Before moving on to the application of tidal streams, and to chartwork in general, there are one or two other basic sources of which you should be aware.

The *Admiralty List of Lights and Fog Signals* is the big-ship equivalent of the information on navigational aids that you will find in yachting almanacs. A point to remember here is that the bearings of lights – for example, to indicate the sector over which a lighthouse shows red or white – are recorded as they appear from seaward.

The Admiralty also publishes a series of **sailing directions or pilots**, authoritative works of reference traditionally famous for their little sketches of the coastline (now replaced by colour photographs) and grim warnings to navigators. But again these are written mainly for ships, not yachts. The *Reeds Almanac* gives detailed pilotage information for approaching and berthing in a wide range of European ports and harbours. Or you may prefer one of the many very detailed pilot books that cover particular areas.

Chartwork

As a qualified Yachtmaster you may choose to navigate electronically, with a multiple-screen chart plotter displaying a radar picture and seabed contours as well as the basic chart, all integrated with the GPS. For the moment, however, we are using a paper chart to explore the basic principles that underlie such equipment. Without this there is nothing to fall back on when the battery goes flat or the electrics are swamped.

Instruments

Essential instruments needed for chartwork:
- Ruler (the longest you can find, preferably made of transparent plastic
- Parallel rule (the roller kind are fine in the classroom, but not on a yacht) for transferring bearings from a compass rose to another part of the chart
- Some sort of course plotter (such as the Breton, the Portland or the Douglas protractor)
- A pair of one-handed dividers for measuring distance (from the latitude scale)
- A pair of compasses for drawing arcs
- A couple of soft hexagonal pencils and a big soft rubber (hard pencils and a small harsh rubber will soon destroy the surface on frequently used corners of the practice chart)

The **symbols** you should use as you come to them are:

⊕	**dead reckoning (DR)**
△	**estimated position (EP)**
⊙	**observed position** or **fix** (position obtained from position lines)
—→—	**water track** (wake course, allowing for leeway)
—»—	**ground track** (course made good relative to land)
—»»—	**tidal stream** or **current**
——→	**position line**
«——»	**transferred position line**
⊞	**GPS waypoint (WPT)**

Nearly all the problems you will be asked to solve on the practice chart are variants of three basic geometrical calculations – fixing the yacht's position, working out the course to reach a given position, and deciding where you have actually arrived after steering a given course for a certain distance. The last of these could theoretically be the **dead reckoning**, which makes no allowance for tidal offset and leeway, but is much more likely to be an **estimated position**, which does makes these allowances.

Eddies

Letter	Morse		Meaning	Letter	Morse		Meaning
ALPHA ● ▬		DIVER	Q ▬ ▬ ● ▬		CUSTOMS
B ▬ ● ● ●		dangerous goods	R ● ▬ ●		—
C ▬ ● ▬ ●		yes	S ● ● ●		astern
D ▬ ● ●		KEEP CLEAR	T ▬		KEEP CLEAR: PAIR TRAWLING
E ●		starboard	U ● ● ▬		DANGER
F ● ● ▬ ●		DISABLED: COMMUNICATE	V ● ● ● ▬		ASSISTANCE NEEDED
G ▬ ▬ ●		pilot needed	W ● ▬ ▬		MEDICAL ASSISTANCE
H ● ● ● ●		pilot on board	X ▬ ● ● ▬		stop and watch
I ● ●		port	Y ▬ ● ▬ ▬		DRAGGING
J ● ▬ ▬ ▬		ON FIRE	Z ▬ ▬ ● ●		tug needed
K ▬ ● ▬		WISH TO COMMUNICATE	1 ● ▬ ▬ ▬ ▬	6 ▬ ● ● ● ●	
L ● ▬ ● ●		STOP	2 ● ● ▬ ▬ ▬	7 ▬ ▬ ● ● ●	
M ▬ ▬		I am stopped	3 ● ● ● ▬ ▬	8 ▬ ▬ ▬ ● ●	
N ▬ ●		no	4 ● ● ● ● ▬	9 ▬ ▬ ▬ ▬ ●	
O ▬ ▬ ▬		MAN OVERBOARD	5 ● ● ● ● ●	0 ▬ ▬ ▬ ▬ ▬	
P ● ▬ ▬ ●		leaving harbour			code flag and answering pennant
			substitutes 1st 2nd 3rd		

Morse Code, the International Code of Signals, and reminders of their joint meanings.
Those in capitals may be worth memorising.

CARDINAL MARKS

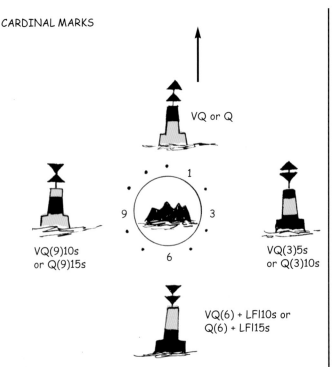

VQ or Q

VQ(9)10s
or Q(9)15s

VQ(3)5s
or Q(3)10s

VQ(6) + LFl10s or
Q(6) + LFl15s

The characteristics of cardinal buoys are easily remembered. The top marks point up (North), down (South), together (West, like a wineglass), and the one with bases together must be East (like an egg). The black sections of the buoy are also where the top marks point. The characteristics of the lights are as on a clock face: three, six and nine. The odd one out – instead of twelve, one.

Special mark – shape optional – has a yellow light (any rhythm)

Isolated danger mark could be a buoy of any shape; light white Gp Fl (2) – remember 2 spheres and Gp Fl (2)

LATERAL MARKS

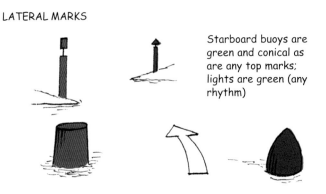

Starboard buoys are green and conical as are any top marks; lights are green (any rhythm)

Lateral buoys are usually related to the flood tide with; port hand buoys are red and flat topped, as are any top marks; lights are red (any rhythm).

Safe water mark can also be a spherical buoy or beacon; light is white isophase, occulting or one long flash every 10 seconds

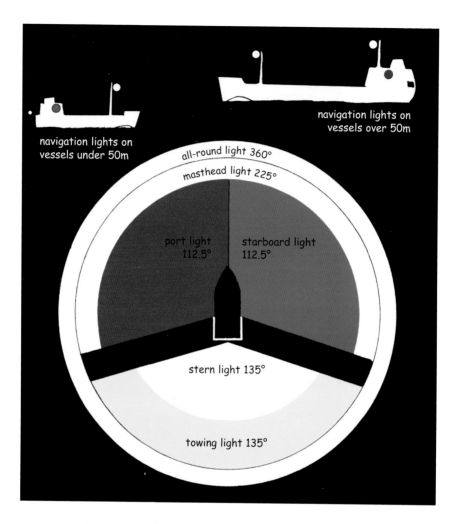

navigation lights on vessels over 50m

navigation lights on vessels under 50m

all-round light 360°

masthead light 225°

port light 112.5°

starboard light 112.5°

stern light 135°

towing light 135°

An easy way to remember the arcs of the navigation lights is that the stern light covers an arc made up of the first three odd numbers - 1, 3, 5 - 135°. Subtract this from 360° and you have the arc of the masthead light - 225°. Halve this and you have the arcs of the port and starboard lights - 112.5°. The all-round light is 360°.

POWER DRIVEN VESSELS UNDER WAY

bow view of vessel less than 50m

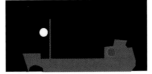

port

stern

bow view of vessel more than 50m

the number of masthead lights - two compulsory over 50m but only one compulsory under 50m - indicate the vessel's length whatever her type

stern

air cushion vessel – bow view

port less than 50m

stern

vessel under 7m - white all-round light

TOWING AND PUSHING

bow

tug less than 50m with length of tow more than 200m

bow tug more than 50m

day signal

stern view, any length

tug more than 50m with length of tow more than 200m

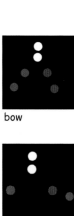

bow

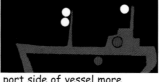

port of vessel less than 50m pushing ahead

stern

bow of vessel less than 50m towing alongside

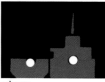

port side of vessel more than 50m

stern

bow

port

sailing vessel making way

stern

FISHING VESSELS

bow of trawler not making way

port side of trawler more than 50m making way

day signal

not making way

surface net fishing vessel making way - port side

stern making way

bow not making way

making way - port side, nets extending more than 150m from vessel

stern making way (additional light shows direction of gear)

day signal

VESSELS NOT UNDER COMMAND OR RESTRICTED IN THEIR ABILITY TO MANOEUVRE

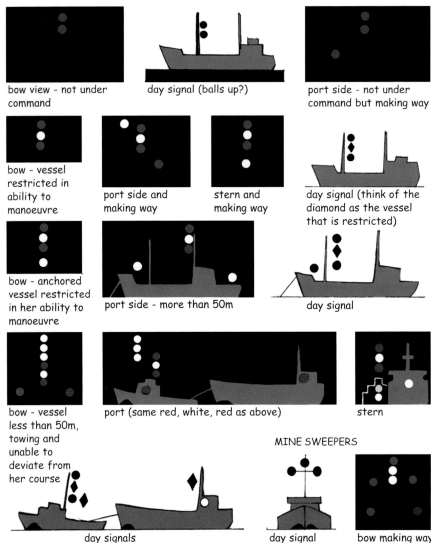

bow view - not under command

day signal (balls up?)

port side - not under command but making way

bow - vessel restricted in ability to manoeuvre

port side and making way

stern and making way

day signal (think of the diamond as the vessel that is restricted)

bow - anchored vessel restricted in her ability to manoeuvre

port side - more than 50m

day signal

bow - vessel less than 50m, towing and unable to deviate from her course

port (same red, white, red as above)

stern

MINE SWEEPERS

day signals

day signal

bow making way

DREDGERS

bow not making way (double red lights indicate obstructed side)

day signal

When the size of the vessel prevents these shapes being shown, a vessel engaged in underwater operations should fly the code flag A

VESSELS CONSTRAINED BY THEIR DRAUGHT

bow

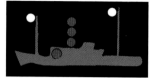
more than 50m – port side

stern

day signal

PILOT VESSELS

bow - at anchor

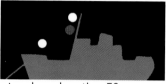
at anchor - less than 50m - port side

stern - making way

more than 50m

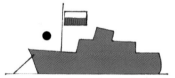
day signal - the red and white of the all-round lights are duplicated in the day signal

ANCHORED VESSELS AND VESSELS AGROUND

at anchor - more than 50m - port side

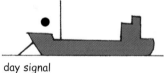
day signal

bow

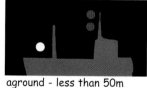
aground - less than 50m

stern

day signal

aground – more than 50m (note preponderance of port red lights)

SEAPLANES

bow

port side

stern

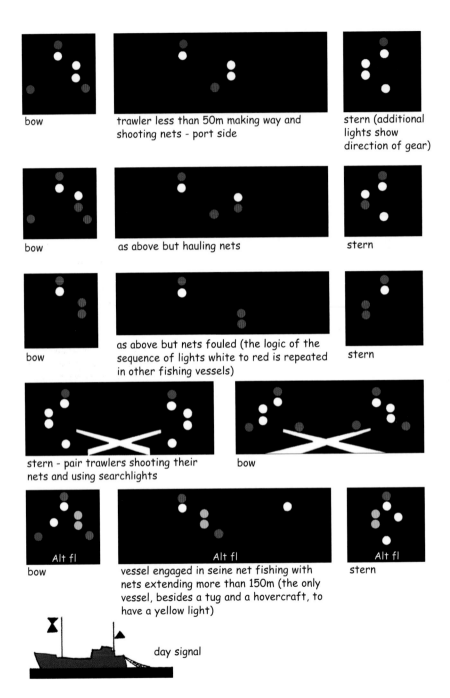

bow

trawler less than 50m making way and shooting nets - port side

stern (additional lights show direction of gear)

bow

as above but hauling nets

stern

bow

as above but nets fouled (the logic of the sequence of lights white to red is repeated in other fishing vessels)

stern

stern - pair trawlers shooting their nets and using searchlights

bow

Alt fl

bow

Alt fl

vessel engaged in seine net fishing with nets extending more than 150m (the only vessel, besides a tug and a hovercraft, to have a yellow light)

Alt fl

stern

day signal

Fixing your position

To obtain a fix you need at least two **position lines**, preferably at a broad angle. These are the lines along which the yacht's position must lie, so that if they intersect, and they are accurate, then there is only one place the boat can be.

The basic **GPS** does this instantly by displaying numerically the lines of latitude and longitude that define your position. Plot them on your chart and you have a **fix**. GPS will also tell you the range and bearing of any waypoint established on a chart (perhaps at the centre of a compass rose, or close to the harbour you are bound for) and programmed into the set by entering its lat and long. You now have another two position lines, producing an even easier fix – the line showing the bearing of the waypoint and the arc indicating its range.

That is the modern way. But there are many other sources of position lines that will confirm or substitute for this electronic device. The most commonly used is the **hand compass bearing** of a visible object marked on the chart – a buoy, a light, or a tower that matches the chartmaker's traditional description 'conspic.'. This may be combined with another compass bearing or with some other source: the extended **transit** between two visible objects; the **distance off** a coastline (as shown, for example, on a radar display, which, with its range rings, is particularly suited to this purpose); the **dipping distance** of a lighthouse at night; a **line of soundings** – or even a single sounding if it establishes a position on a clearly defined seabed contour. In an emergency, the Coastguard may be able to give the bearing of your VHF radio transmission.

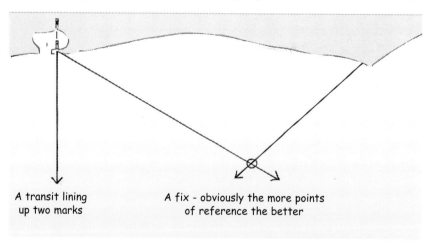

A transit lining
up two marks

A fix - obviously the more points
of reference the better

Position lines for a fix can be obtained from a compass bearing,
a transit, distance off, or a line of soundings.

Using a couple of position lines is the principle you instinctively apply when sailing past, say, a pier, and you think: 'We're about two miles off, steering roughly parallel with the shore, and the pier's abeam, so we must be about . . . there on the chart'.

A common dodge for improving on guesswork for the distance off is known as **doubling the angle on the bow**. If you take a bearing of an object on the shore ahead and then maintain a steady course until the angle between bearing and course has doubled (see diagram), the three lines plotted on the chart form a triangle with two equal sides. Equipped with a log and a tidal atlas, you know the length of one of those sides – the distance the yacht has covered – and that is also the distance off.

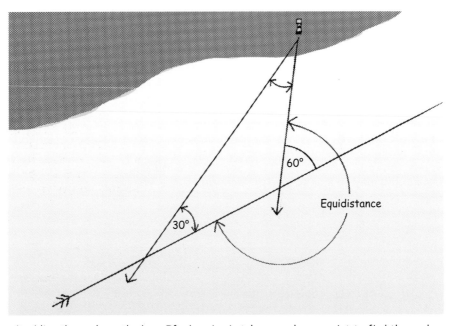

Doubling the angle on the bow. If a bearing is taken on a known point to find the angle it makes from the ship's bow (in this case 30°) and another taken when that figure is doubled (ie 60°), the distance between the two points from which the bearings were taken will be the same as the ship's distance from the known point.

One combination of position lines that ships used before the days of radar, and which can still be useful aboard a yacht, is the **bearing of a lighthouse at night and its dipping distance**. As we all know, the curvature of the earth makes distant objects fall below the horizon. And the distance at which this

Position of tabulated tidal stream

happens to a lighthouse of a given height, plus the observer's own height above sea level, can be found from tables provided in nautical almanacs. The position line obtained in this way is a circle round the light whose radius is that total distance. A compass bearing of the light, intersecting the circle, gives a fix.

Two points to remember about this calculation

- The charted height of a lighthouse is measured from MHWS, so if it is not high water you have to add on the difference between that and the actual tidal level before consulting the distance table.
- Do not be caught out by the examiner suggesting the use of dipping distance when the yacht is still beyond the light's luminous range.

A general warning about compass bearings – avoid taking them from objects like headlands and hills; these may look clearcut from seaward, but their precise location on a two-dimensional chart is difficult to establish. Also, to reiterate a point made earlier, avoid shallow angles between bearings because they increase the margin of error. Remember too that a **back bearing** from something you have passed may be just as useful as one taken from an object you are approaching – although, in practice, people often forget to look behind them.

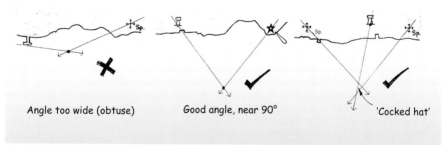

Angle too wide (obtuse)   Good angle, near 90°   'Cocked hat'

Right and wrong fix. A right angle between bearings reduces the margin of error. Very broad – or narrow – angles increase it.

Radar fixes

The combination of a radar display's range marker and (relative) bearing line – whose primary use is collision avoidance, because a constant bearing means you are on a collision course – can be used to fix your position on a chart. If the set has a movable cursor, the required information will be automatically shown. However this presupposes that the radar picture can be accurately reconciled with the features shown on your chart – not always easy. In any case, the recommended technique is to play to the radar's strength by measuring a series of ranges, rather than bearings, to fix your position where the arcs cross.

Cocked hats and running fixes

However carefully you deploy your **hand bearing compass**, visual bearings will almost always be inaccurate – as you will clearly be reminded when three of them are plotted to produce not a precise intersection, but a triangular **'cocked hat'**. Your boat is probably in the middle of it, but if the position is critical, assume the worst case – or take fresh bearings.

'Ease her down Joe, I've just lost the leading marks.'

Cold front

Even if only one identifiable object is visible, it may be possible to establish what is known as a **running fix**, by taking two successive bearings. The first is plotted and the log mileage at that time recorded. After a suitable interval a second bearing of the same object is taken, and the course made good during the interval – allowing for the tidal stream – is plotted from any point on the first bearing or position line. This first line is then transferred (see diagram) so as to mark the only point on the second line where the track made good actually fits between the two bearings. That must be the yacht's position.

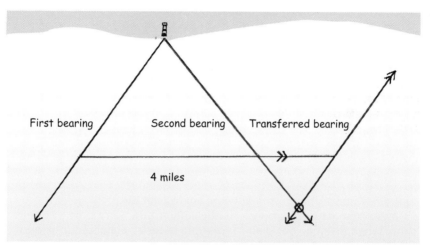

A running fix. Take a bearing from a known point and plot it on the chart. Then run a recorded distance (4 miles in this example) and take a second bearing. Transfer the first bearing 4 miles to intersect the second. Your fix is where the two position lines cross.

Transits

A transit (preferably between objects a good distance apart) can be extremely useful just on its own. The classic application is a pair of **leading marks** or leading lights to show the safest way into a harbour or the best water over a difficult bar. To take other examples of which RYA examiners are fond: two objects might be chosen so that as long as one is kept 'open' of the other (that is, not in transit), the yacht will stay clear of sandbanks lining the entrance to a bay; or the appearance of a transit might be used as a kind of visual alarm clock, to remind the helmsman when to change course. Remember it takes only a moment to record a transit with the time it appeared – it may suddenly be needed.

Pilotage

This kind of navigation – the sort you need when first leaving harbour to explore the local coastline, conducted visually from the cockpit with quick references to the chart – comes under the heading of **pilotage**. The techniques are simple, but can sometimes be difficult to apply. Finding your way into a rock strewn estuary on a swirling tide, for example, may involve rapid changes of course with only a small margin of error. So you need some sort of **pilotage plan**, and if your plan is at all complicated **write it down** – on a single sheet of paper in a plastic cover you can take into the cockpit.

When 'buoy hopping' in bad weather or poor visibility, it is extremely helpful, when you reach each mark, to have pre-plotted and noted the bearing – and distance – of the next. As the boat lurches round and the boom crashes over, you immediately know where to steer and where to look (something the GPS would also tell you, incidentally, if the relevant waypoint had already been entered).

The hand bearing compass often plays a part, to provide **turning points** and/or **clearing lines** – the maximum or minimum bearings that will lead you clear of dangerous rock or shoals. But when making your plan, look first for **transits** between a couple of prominent marks, as discussed earlier, because these may give you a course to steer without reference to anything but your own eyes. Hence, of course, the value of purpose-built leading marks to bring vessels safely into harbour – the ultimate aid to pilotage.

If it is a commercial harbour – particularly a busy ferry port – consult an almanac when making your plan to note the **harbour signals** controlling ships entering or leaving. And remember that big vessels 'constrained by their draft' or otherwise disinclined to get out of your way, may have to be avoided. Plot your approach to keep outside the deep water channel.

The **echo sounder** (preferably with an alarm) may well be helpful, both to warn of shallow water and provide a quick check of your position above the seabed contours.

If there are buoys along your track, steer fairly close to them (unless of course they mark an isolated danger). In poor visibility, especially, you may need to be doubly sure you are passing the correct one by reading its name or number. You can then set off on the next leg from a confirmed position (though not necessarily an absolutely precise one, since a big tidal range will move the buoy about). As you pass the buoy, the water swirling round it is an excellent tidal stream indicator.

Yacht harbour, marina

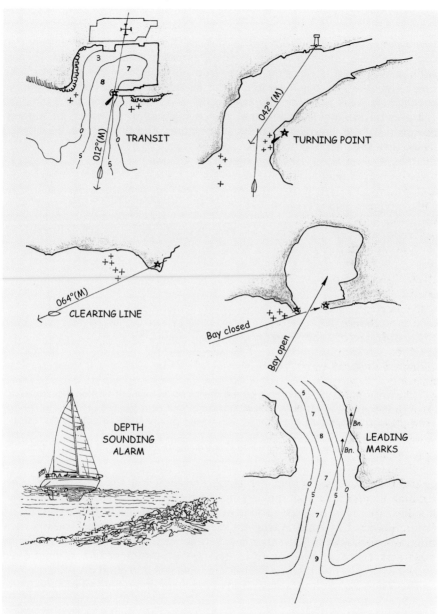

- TRANSIT — 012°(M)
- TURNING POINT — 042°(M)
- CLEARING LINE — 064°(M)
- Bay closed / Bay open
- DEPTH SOUNDING ALARM
- LEADING MARKS — Bn. Bn.

Pilotage uses many visual aids and techniques to help you to navigate safely inshore.

Plotting a course

If you steer due north by your boat's compass then it is extremely unlikely that you will actually travel in a true northerly direction over the ground. To start with, the compass is pointing not to true north, but to the magnetic pole (the variation we discussed earlier), and it almost certainly has some additional deviation. If yours is a sailing boat with the wind ahead or on the beam, she will also be making leeway – that is, moving slightly crabwise, perhaps 5° downwind of the direction her bows are pointing. And she will also be affected by the tidal stream.

Much of the chartwork in this part of the course would be much simpler if there were no such things as tidal streams. These may carry your boat bodily sideways – as if on a moving carpet – and turn the straight line of your course into a potentially confusing triangle of velocities. In practice, the actual course may be a shallow curve. Charts and tidal atlases enable the navigator to shape a course and plot it to allow for tide.

The tide may simply help her along or cancel out some of her progress through the water (a boat moving at 4½ knots with a 1½ knot tide under her travels twice as fast over the ground as the same boat heading into the tide – 6 knots instead of 3 – which is why it is so important for small craft to work their tides). However, the stream sometimes sets across your course, altering hour by hour, and this has to be allowed for (along with the other factors mentioned above) when **plotting the ground track**, or course made good over the ground.

The following method is illustrated in the diagram on the top of page 35:
1   Add or subtract deviation to convert compass course (C) to magnetic (M).
2   Subtract westerly variation to convert magnetic course (M) to true (T).

Fix

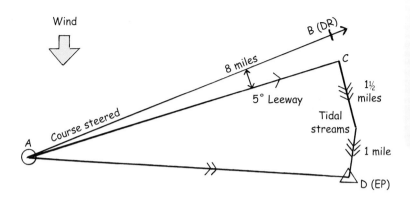

Plotting a course.

3 Lay off the resulting true course steered from the observed position A; measure the distance run through the water against the adjacent latitude scale (in this example 8 miles in 2 hours) and mark it off to give position B – the 'dead reckoning'.
4 Apply leeway downwind (in this example 5°) and label the resulting water track to position C.
5 Look up the direction and rate of the tidal stream during these same two hours and lay them off from C as two successive '**vectors**', one for each hour, so as to establish the estimated position D.
6 Connect A and D to give an approximation of the yacht's track and complete the 'velocity triangle'.

The accuracy of the estimated position will depend on, among other things, the accuracy of the helmsman's steering, the allowance for leeway (which varies with the type of boat and the set of the sails), the log reading, and the tidal stream predictions – so, as you can see, small boat navigation is definitely not an exact science.

Shaping a course from one given position to another

In a sense this is the same triangular problem in reverse: anticipating the effect of tide and leeway instead of working it out after the event. Again the method is shown in the diagram on page 36 (notice – because this is often a source of misunderstanding – that the yacht's progress along her track AB is *not* measured off from the starting point A, but from the end of the tidal vector C):

'Relax – I've got a back bearing that clears everything.'

1 Lay off the desired ground track from A to B.
2 Calculate roughly how long the trip will take (in this example, something over two hours) and lay off the appropriate tidal vectors to point C.
3 With compasses set to the distance the yacht will cover during the same two hours, strike an arc from C through the desired ground track AB and mark it D, so that CD is the water track required to reach the nearest practical point to B.
4 Compare the water track with the magnetic compass rose and label it.
5 Apply the appropriate corrections for leeway and deviation (both of which you will be given in an exam) to obtain the compass course to steer.

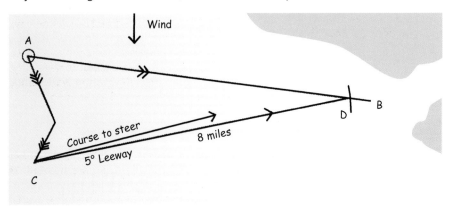

Shaping a course.

Rock awash at chart datum

This rather clumsy procedure actually takes the yacht in a shallow meandering curve from A to D. If it is necessary to stay close to the track from A to B – for example, to avoid straying into shallow water – each hour's tidal stream could be plotted to produce a separate course to steer. Alternatively, as here, a succession of tidal vectors can be plotted end to end to produce a single mean course to steer for the whole trip. As you near B, so you must plot your EP and adjust course to hit it off exactly – or to be safe, aim a bit uptide.

GPS, through its cross track function, is making similar sorts of calculation all the time, without knowing why. Having entered B as a waypoint, the size and direction of the cross track error (XTE) tells you what course correction to apply. If the GPS waypoint bearing remains constant, you are on a 'collision course', which may or may not be a good thing, depending on what the waypoint represents. Again, if it's important to stay on track because of nearby hazards, it may help to plot a **cross track error 'ladder'** on the chart – a long grid marked with distances from the waypoint and either side of the track, so that you can instantly interpret the numbers on the GPS display. But, as with any electronic aid to navigation, it obviously pays to have an independent means of estimating your position from time to time, until eventually you get a visual bearing or transit from your destination.

There are some simple cases – for example, a passage across the North Sea or the Channel that is expected to last about 12 hours, with a fair wind – when it is actually more efficient to ignore the tide. Rather than fight to stay on the direct ground track, it will pay you to steer a direct course through the water, allowing the yacht to be swept first to one side of the track and then the other by the tide, in an S-shaped curve whose shape is related to the tidal curves mentioned earlier. This assumes that the effects of the tidal ebb and flow roughly cancel out.

In other situations the tide should be allowed for positively. For example, when tacking across a tidal stream, it pays to set off up-tide, so you are lifted up to windward by it – a tactic known as **'lee-bowing'**. The boat's sideways movement will free the apparent wind.

Allowing for a tidal stream is also crucial when tacking across the tide to clear a headland or round a buoy, as you often do when racing. If necessary, plot the ground track required by applying a tidal correction to the water track dictated by the wind, then go about when you come on to that bearing.

Electronic navigation

As we saw earlier when describing individual navigational aids, the two main pieces of equipment which make electronic navigation possible are the **Global Positioning System (GPS)** and the **chart plotter**.

GPS interrogates a network of US military satellites orbiting the earth (European and Russian systems are under development) to calculate your Lat and Long to within a few metres and then constantly update that position. It uses the same technology as a car's 'satnav' – but without the bossy voice telling you which way to steer.

In its simplest maritime guise, a handheld GPS resembles a mobile phone. Integrated with an electronic chart it creates the chart plotter, displaying the yacht's moving position – where you are and how you got there. It can also be linked to a VHF radio which in an emergency (See Safety and seagoing practice, page 94) will automatically relay the yacht's identity and position to rescue services ashore. Using closely related technology, the chart plotter can in turn be integrated with an automatic identification system (**AIS**) displaying the movements of all large vessels (and other yachts linked to the system).

Any navigator presented with such a remarkable resource might be tempted to believe that it makes traditional methods redundant. GPS has certainly been eagerly adopted by sailors, to a point where it is nowadays regarded as the 'normal' means of navigation.

However in truth it is just another electronic aid – albeit an extremely powerful one – that can be deliberately degraded by the Pentagon (as it was in earlier years), or rendered useless by a flat battery. And that is how RYA instructors will regard GPS for the foreseeable future – indeed you may find there is an exam question illustrating the dangers of relying too heavily on electronic equipment.

GPS is not intelligent. It does not think. It will tell you the bearing and distance of a given waypoint, but not how to get there safely. To take an exaggerated example – if asked for the course from Plymouth to Swansea, your GPS would direct you across Dartmoor! More realistically, it might tempt you to lay a straight course across a dangerous shoal when traditional paper chartwork –

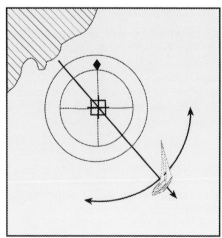

Position lines from a GPS waypoint.

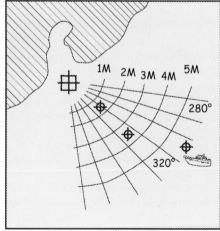

GPS plotting web for fast craft.

GPS waypoint

or indeed a chart plotter, when correctly used and accurately calibrated – would prompt you to avoid it.

A more subtle temptation could arise when crossing a strong tidal stream to reach a harbour sheltering, say, behind an off-lying reef. By plotting a way-point in the entrance and then simply steering the continuously changing course suggested by GPS, you would be making a big sweep down tide – which could lead into danger. The traditional method of offsetting the tide (See 'Shaping a course') would be both safer and more efficient.

The navigator of a fast power boat might respond that bouncing along at 20 knots, he does not have that much time to spend at the chart table. One answer may be to pre-plot a 'web' of distances and bearings from the relevant waypoint (see diagram on page 38), on which readings of bearing and range from the GPS display (BRG, RNG) can quickly be noted. And of course you could also slow down.

Whatever method is used, the underlying navigational principles do not change. As we saw earlier, the numerical GPS readings of Lat and Long, range and bearing are simply additional sources of position lines, any two of which will give you a fix. One method should be used to back up the other, even if you normally rely on a dedicated chart plotter. An electrical fault or a dead battery could otherwise leave you helpless.

For example it takes only seconds to take a visual bearing or note a transit that confirms an electronic display. And it is just as easy to punch in the wrong Lat and Long co-ordinates of a GPS waypoint as it is to dial a wrong telephone number, particularly if they are entered straight from a directory or pilot book. The waypoint's range and bearing should always therefore be confirmed by checking that they match your estimated position on the chart.

Points to remember when using GPS

- GPS gives you the *direct* course to a waypoint, not necessarily the *safe* course – it doesn't notice rocks in the way and it doesn't allow for tidal streams.
- A waypoint placed at the centre of a compass rose gives you a read-out of bearing and distance – this may be quicker than plotting Lat and Long.
- Never enter waypoints straight from a directory or pilot book without plotting them on the chart.
- Make sure you have entered a waypoint's Lat and Long *correctly*, by checking that its bearing and distance match your estimated position.
- Don't plot a waypoint exactly at a buoy or beacon – you might collide with it!

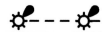

If you have the necessary patience, **a series of waypoints** can be programmed in to provide a complete route along which the GPS will guide you. A word of caution, though – plot the waypoints near, but not actually on top of a buoy or a pierhead, otherwise the instruction that you have 'arrived at your destination' could be accompanied by a nasty breaking sound.

A waypoint is also a valuable source of position lines, as well as an intermediate destination. In this second role, a waypoint can be placed quite arbitrarily – but preferably at the centre of the chart's compass rose – so as to give its bearing (position line 1) and distance from the yacht (position line 2). This may well be quicker than plotting Lat and Long.

A **chart plotter** does the job even more quickly. Besides showing the yacht's position, it can have a **movable cursor**, whose bearing and distance are automatically displayed. Place the cursor on your destination, or outside a shoal you want to avoid, and you instantly have a preliminary course to steer, a clearing line or whatever. Installed in the cockpit, this complex electronic device can therefore become almost an extension of the most basic form of navigation – visual pilotage.

In summary, **electronic and traditional navigation are not exclusive alternatives**, and should not be treated as such. A passage chart provides a broad picture to complement the variable focus of a chart plotter. A hand bearing compass visually confirms the identity of an object marked by the chart plotter's cursor. GPS shows speed over the ground to set alongside the traditional log's speed through the water. One method complements the other – and also provides an essential back-up.

Log keeping

There are many different reasons for keeping a log, among them the possibility of GPS failure or the sudden onset of fog, and various types of log result. A motor yacht's log, for example, might include a record of rpm, temperature, charging rate and fuel state that would not be needed aboard a sailing vessel. The universal requirement is always to have some way of plotting the yacht's position, or reworking a doubtful calculation, from a basic record of time, course, speed, navigational marks and so on. On a large vessel where the crew is organised into watches, a log also helps to tell the new watch what has been happening while they were below. In any case, potential Yachtmasters need a record of their seatime to obtain that important certificate!

Leading lights

Passage planning

Getting out the charts to plan and anticipate a passage can be great fun (better than the real thing in some cases!) as well as saving time and trouble at sea.

Having made sure the boat itself is properly prepared, with adequate fuel, water and safety equipment, the first item on your check list is those **charts**. You will probably need several of them – a small scale chart covering the whole passage, one or more detailed charts on a larger scale, and perhaps a harbour plan of your destination – which will probably be found in a **pilot book** of the area. A **weather forecast** is obviously going to be helpful. And you will certainly need **tide tables**, preferably supplemented by a tidal stream atlas.

Tides may well be a critical factor in your planning, especially in areas like the Bristol Channel where there is a big tidal range. On any coastal trip, a lot of time can be saved by working your tides – carrying a favourable stream for more than six hours, arriving at a navigational corner like the North Foreland as the tide turns in your favour, or arranging coastal hops to avoid hitting the ferocious Portland race at full bore.

Passage planning checklist

- Small-scale chart – choose best route to avoid hazards, optimise times and landfall
- Large-scale charts and harbour plans – for destination and possible diversions
- Note times of HW and LW; check tidal streams
- Note relevant waypoints, light characteristics, harbour signals, limiting depths, clearing lines
- Calculate fuel requirements
- Plot initial track

If your destination is a river entrance with a tricky bar, you will need a safe minimum depth (time to use those tidal curves or the 'rule of twelfths') and it will be far better to arrive on the flood than on the ebb. The same goes for crossing the shallow swatchways of the Thames Estuary.

Of course sooner or later, however cunning your plan, you will have to buck a foul tide. The trick is to make positive use of the unfavourable periods by putting in, say, to refuel, to enjoy a meal ashore, or just to have a rest. Sailing across strong tides will test your chartwork, although on some of the commonly used cross-Channel and North Sea passages the tidal streams roughly cancel out. On longer passages, navigators often try to arrange their landfall

5_2

for just before dawn, so as to make use of the lights to give a reliable fix, then enter harbour in daylight. Going foreign, you must inform Customs if you are sailing directly to or from a port outside the EC or if you have goods to declare – such as animals.

Any preparation that can be made in advance, before leaving harbour, will make things easier at sea – programming the GPS, looking up harbour signals and VHF channels, noting the times of high water, plotting a couple of likely courses – perhaps including an 'escape route' in the event of gear failure or a sudden bad weather – and so on. Every passage will probably have one or more critical points – perhaps crossing a difficult bar, anticipating a break in the weather, using the tide, or making an unfamiliar landfall. Build your plan round them.

Points to remember about navigation

- Never miss an easy chance to fix your position, eg from a transit.
- Try never to waste a favourable tide – it could double your speed.
- Cardinal buoys follow the clock face, and lateral ones match your navigation lights.
- Variation West, Compass Best.
- The Rule of Twelfths – 1, 2, 3, 3, 2, 1.
- Pilotage often involves rapid changes of course and perspective – prepare a written, cockpit-proof plan.
- Electronic and traditional navigation are complementary, not mutually exclusive.

Wreck, depth found by sounding

Weather

Apart from the sheer pleasure of understanding our daily weather, the study of meteorology is obviously extremely important for sailors.

On passage, we need to recognise the first signs of an approaching depression, with its rain, gales and wind shifts. When racing inshore, we have to make use of more local effects, like the summer sea breezes. Preparing for Yachtmaster exams, we also need to know something of meteorological theory, with its special language. We may even want to draw our own weather maps.

Fortunately, much of the forecasters' technical jargon is already familiar from the newspaper weather maps, radio and television. Indeed, the BBC shipping forecast is almost a national institution! We are used to looking at patterns of 'isobars' or hearing about 'advancing depressions' and 'associated troughs'. There are even satellite pictures of the swirling clouds that mark their progress. With this background, the meteorology section of the RYA course is simply a matter of going back to first principles and working through them coherently, learning the definitions as you go.

The basic weather system and terms used

In describing the weather, the most fundamental distinction we make is between a warm day and a cold one. And, in truth, temperature ultimately determines the other characteristics that interest us – whether it is wet or dry, sunny or cloudy, windy or calm.

In north-west Europe we live roughly on the boundary of the cold air masses of the polar regions and the warm air of the tropics. The line where they meet is known as the **polar front**.

The density of air varies with its temperature, so a warm pocket of air tends to float to the top of the surrounding cooler mass, just as a cold pocket of air descends. The movement set up by this tendency for warmer air to rise – sometimes a complete circulation – is known as **convection**. As the air rises it cools, which is one way that the invisible vapour carried by any air, but especially warm air – which can carry more of it – condenses into visible droplets of cloud or fog. Convective cumulus cloud, which is the fluffy white kind seen in children's picture books, is a result of this process. Any other cooling process will have a similar effect, although the visual result may be quite different.

In other words, the amount of water vapour that air can absorb before it becomes saturated increases with temperature. As cooling air reaches this varying point of saturation, it is said to be at the **dew point**. If it gets any cooler, the excess water vapour will condense.

The warm moist air inside your car mists over a cold windscreen because the glass cools it below its dew point. More relevantly, warm moist air advancing from subtropical regions across colder northern seas – from the Azores into the Western Approaches, for example – will tend to release its excess moisture as fog. This consists of water droplets, just like the convective cloud, but we give it a different name because the air from which it condenses is cooler than the mass above. There is no convective tendency to rise, so the fog characteristically drifts near the surface.

In general, a mixed air mass, with the cooler, denser air at the bottom, is going to be stable. One with warmer, less dense air temporarily trapped at its base will be unstable – a characteristic of polar air masses moving south over warmer seas. So the polar front, along which moving air masses of different temperatures tend to meet and swirl, is also likely to be an area of complex instability.

A **depression**, the most prominent single feature of the weather along the coastlines of north-west Europe, often starts as no more than a ripple on the polar front way out in the Atlantic. A bulge of warm subtropical air pushes into and over a cooler northern air mass and begins to swirl upwards. The bulge becomes a moving wave, with a **warm front** on its leading edge, and a **cold front** on its trailing edge as cooler air closes in behind it. And if, as often happens, the cold front eventually overtakes the warm front, cutting off its supply of warm air, the fronts are said to be **occluded**.

The depression, centred on the crest of the wave, is therefore an area of ascending air and low pressure, and commonly referred to simply as a 'low'. A complete area of relatively high pressure, where cool air is gently descending, is known as an **anticyclone** (the opposite word, cyclone, being reserved for vigorous tropical depressions) or just a '**high**'.

Pressure can be measured with a **barometer** (the compact aneroid kind is the type most usually found on yachts) and shown on a scale divided into millibars. The pressures we are concerned with fluctuate around the 1000 millibar level, with less than 940 millibars in a really deep 'low', and more than 1040 millibars in an intense 'high' (that is a 100 millibar range). Two lows are often said to be divided by a **ridge of high pressure**. Within a depression, pressure is especially low along the line of the two fronts, which are therefore important examples of what is known as a **trough**.

Meteorologists illustrate and analyse these features by drawing maps, **synoptic charts**, covered in isobars – that is, lines of equal barometric pressure. The effect is to show the contours of a depression or anticyclone, just as height contours on a land map show the shape of a range of hills.

On a weather map they also show the direction of the wind, because in the northern hemisphere **air circulates anticlockwise round a depression**, along the contours but slightly inwards towards the centre, while round an anticyclone it circulates in the opposite direction: clockwise and slightly outwards.

The contours of a depression tend to be steeper than those of an anti-cyclone, especially near its centre, and this shows up on the map in the closer spacing of the isobars. The winds are correspondingly stronger, often up to gale force and beyond, which is of course why yachtsmen should be on their guard against the approach of a deep low. In any case, the rain and drizzle that usually accompany its passing fronts put it in the general category of bad weather, whereas a stationary anticyclone is often the source of a fine spell of summer weather.

Not all depressions come in from the Atlantic. For example, in hot summer weather a thundery low sometimes forms in France and spreads across the Channel to bring its clouds into southern England. But the classic pattern of British weather – and certainly the one most relevant to passing the Yachtmaster meteorology exam – is caused by a depression tracking north-east across the British Isles until it disappears somewhere over the Baltic. The clouds that signal its approach, the falling barometer, the **wind shifts** marking its con-tours – these are all the basis of those old weather sayings about mackerel skies, the moon hiding her head in a halo, and winds that shift against the sun.

Look at an isobaric chart of a symmetrical low, and you will see that if it passes directly overhead, moving north-east, the wind will shift through 180° after a brief lull – roughly from south-east to north-west (in our diagram on page 40, the observer's viewpoint moves along track A). If the centre of low pressure passes to the north (track B), a southerly wind will **veer – that is, shift in a clockwise direction** – until it becomes westerly. If the low passes to the south (track C), the wind will **back – anticlockwise** – from an easterly to a northerly direction. The barometer will fall and rise during the same period.

If you draw the chart a little more realistically to show the deeper troughs of low pressure accompanying the advancing warm and cold fronts, the wind shifts will be sharper at these points, especially at the passage of the cold front. And if this primary low has a secondary one developing on the tail of the cold front – perhaps more violent than its parent – the wind may back sharply only to veer again:

> *When the wind shifts against the sun,*
> *Trust it not for back 'twill run.*

Patterns of falling and rising pressure can be traced in the same way, for example at the cold front:

> *When rise commences after low,*
> *Squalls expect and then clear blow.*

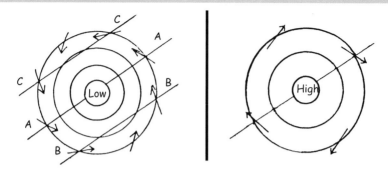

Above: The basic wind patterns of 'low'
and 'high' in the northern hemisphere.
Below: Additional features in
practice – fronts, and a secondary depression.

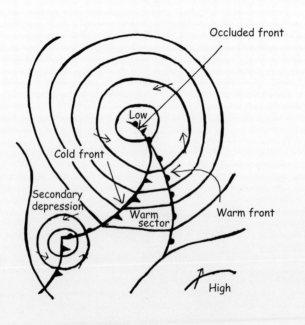

Ground track

But the first signs of an approaching depression are likely to be visual – the wispy 'mares' tails' driven far ahead of it by strong, high altitude winds:

> *Mackerel sky and mares' tails,*
> *Make tall ships carry small sails.*

Clouds

Meteorologists distinguish clouds according to their height and form, using the **Latin words cumulus** (heap), **stratus** (blanket), and **cirrus** (curl of hair) to describe heaped-up, layered and high wispy cloud respectively. The word **alto** may be added to indicate a medium-level cloud of some particular form, and **nimbus** (storm cloud) means rain-bearing. But the resulting classification is not totally logical, so you just have to learn the main types.

Clouds to remember

- **Cumulus (Cu)** – low, mainly white clouds piled into small heaps, usually associated with fine weather.
- **Stratocumulus (Sc)** – low heaped clouds gathered into an extensive layer.
- **Cumulonimbus (Cb)** – towering heaps of cloud that produce showers or thunderstorms.
- **Stratus (St)** – low layer of featureless grey cloud.
- **Nimbostratus (Ns)** – layers of dark rain-bearing cloud.
- **Altocumulus (Ac)** – medium-level heaped clouds in rounded, lens-shaped or castellated form.
- **Altostratus (As)** – medium-level layer of cloud through which 'watery' sun may be seen.
- **Cirrus (Ci)** – high-level streaks of cloud formed by ice crystals, often referred to as 'mares' tails'.
- **Cirrocumulus (Cc)** – high-level heaped clouds which may assume regular rippled pattern (usually benign) of a 'mackerel sky'.
- **Cirrostratus (Cs)** – high-level layered cloud which may produce a 'halo' round the sun or moon.

Clouds are generally confined to the troposphere. That is the first 45,000 feet or so of the earth's atmosphere, within which the temperature falls as you go higher. Near the top of it, strong jet stream winds of 100 mph or more often blow in the direction a depression is moving, carrying the high-level clouds associated with it far ahead of the lower, heavier clouds that bring the rain. Cirrus clouds, therefore, are often a sign of approaching bad weather:

> *If clouds look as if scratched by a hen,*
> *Get ready to reef your topsails then.*

Such clouds are formed by showers of tiny ice crystals, which fall through the strong upper winds and appear to trail in one direction or another as their lateral movement slows down. The white streaks (the tips of the 'mares' tails') therefore point back towards the centre of low pressure advancing behind them. They also enable you to apply what is known as the **crossed wind rule**. This means that if you stand with your back to the surface wind and the clouds show that the upper wind is coming from your left, then the weather is prob-

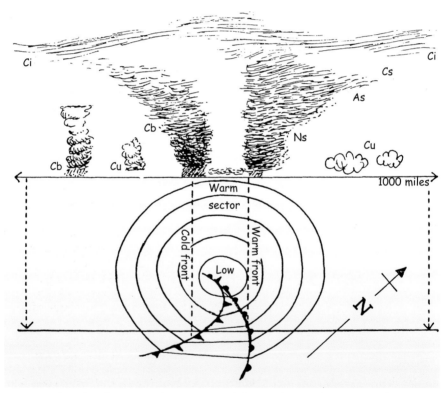

A section through a depression showing types of cloud and areas of rain. Most depressions are more complex than this, but the basic features can usually be recognised.

Estimated position

ably deteriorating. This is related to 'Buys Ballots Law' – if you stand with your back to the wind (in the northern hemisphere) low pressure will be on your left.

Two other types of cloud that characterise a passing frontal depression are cirrostratus and cumulonimbus. In cirrostratus, the layered ice crystals often produce a warning halo effect round the sun or moon as a clear sky clouds over. In cumulonimbus, the tall clouds produce heavy rain showers as the unstable, blustery cold front comes through. However, by the time a complete low pressure system has come and gone, nearly all the cloud types will probably have been represented.

Depressions

A large depression may easily be 1000 miles in extent, with cloud stretching 500 miles ahead of the warm front. Its speed of movement may be anything up to 60 knots – one of the hazards of weather forecasting – so you can see that it can take all day for the first warning cloud signs to be translated into the rain and turbulence of the frontal areas. Not that every depression produces rain. However, assuming a vigorous low, with two distinct frontal troughs in the classic form, the belt of rain along the warm front may be about 100 miles wide, and the cold front's rain belt perhaps 50 miles wide.

Two useful ways of visualising a depression

- Look down on the isobars of the familiar **weather map** and imagine two big swirls of cloud accompanying the fronts, as sometimes seen quite clearly on satellite pictures.
- Take a vertical **cross-section**, which is most usefully drawn (as in our illustration) along a SW–NE axis that cuts across the two fronts.

Now imagine the whole system tracking north-east. The map shows the shifting wind directions as felt by a more or less stationary yacht on the surface, the likely strength of the wind (**remember – the closer the isobars, the stronger the wind**), and the rise and fall of the barometer.

The cross-section shows the advancing warm front with the succession of cloud formations that precede it, the warm sector, and the wedge of cold air closing in behind it.

As the depression approaches, the wind will back southerly and the classic progression of clouds will probably appear: high wispy streaks of cloud (cirrus) spreading to shroud the sun (cirrostratus) and then steadily lowering and darkening (altostratus and nimbostratus) until the rain begins to fall – light at first, but soon settling into a continuous moderately heavy spell as the warm sector arrives. Meanwhile, the wind will have increased.

Entering the warm sector, fog or drizzle may reduce visibility even though the rain has eased. The temperature will rise (although the generally damp conditions will probably disguise this). The most significant effect for yachtsmen may well be the veering wind, which should then stay steady until the arrival of the cold front, when it will veer again towards the north-west, usually more sharply. The barometer will reflect the same pattern – steady, then rising rapidly.

If the low is a vigorous one, with steep pressure gradients (closely spaced isobars) and correspondingly strong winds (a fall in pressure of 5–6 millibars in three hours is considered 'rapid'), this is when they will be felt. The **cold front** is not only likely to bring heavy rain squalls, but its generally gusty winds will accentuate the cooler, fresher atmosphere. Towering thundery clouds may even produce some hail. At least a cold front tends to pass more quickly than its warm counterpart. The cloud sequence may now to some extent be reversed, but most important is the brisk process of heaped-up medium-level clouds (cumulus or cumulonimbus) with clear blue sky soon showing above.

On land it is a cheerful moment – the arrival of 'showers and bright periods' after a spell of miserable wet weather. At sea, it may mean pulling down the last reef and weathering the worst of the blow.

Anticyclones

For sailors, and those on land, **high pressure generally means fine weather**. The pressure gradients around an anticyclone are usually less steep than in a depression, so light winds are the rule and gales are a rarity. While the air continues to descend in the high, diverging outwards to feed the inward circulation of any neighbouring lows, it is compressed, warmed and dried. Moisture picked up from the cold sea may condense out, but at this low level the incipient cloud is often stifled by a temperature inversion – this is a layer of warm air sitting on top of the cooler surface air in which the cloud starts to form. Anticyclonic weather may therefore be dull and foggy, but it seldom rains.

Local weather

For the short time that most yachtsmen are at sea, local weather – such as sea breezes, violent squalls or fog – can be just as important as the big weather systems we have already mentioned.

Coastal **sea breezes** are produced in summer when rising air above the rapidly heated land surface sucks in air from offshore. These breezes reach

Flashing light (Fl) – dark period exceeds light

their peak on a hot afternoon, perhaps as much as force 4–5 (but not more), and die away at sunset. They are confined to within a few miles of the coast-line, where a line of convective cumulus clouds over the land may indicate that such a breeze is developing. The first boat to pick this up could win the club handicap race by half a mile!

At night, when the land cools more rapidly than the sea (whose tempera-ture scarcely changes) the reverse process may produce a **land breeze**, but it tends to be a weak affair by comparison. Where convection is more violent, round the base of a towering thunder cloud for example, the thermal up-draught can cause sudden **squalls** and localised wind shifts (if in any doubt, shorten sail quickly). The opposite sort of instability, when cold air rolls down the sides of a coastal valley or fjord, accentuating the night-time tendency to a land breeze, is called a **katabatic wind**.

For the racing yachtsman, the smallest of local effects – up-draughts, down-draughts, wind shadows, eddies in the lee of a headland, or the tendency for surface winds to back as they cross land – are worth anticipating. On the other hand, those cruising can sometimes pay too much anxious attention to weather forecasts. Unless you are in the Yachtmaster exam room, you only need be on the lookout for the few real dangers: a sudden deep low is one of them; fog in a crowded shipping lane is another.

Fog

The basic cause of fog, as we saw earlier, is air cooling to the critical tempera-ture (the dew point) below which it can no longer hold all its moisture as invis-ible vapour. Surplus vapour then condenses out as water droplets suspended in the air. The resulting fog is given various names, depending on the circum-stances. Frontal fog, for example, occurs where warm and cold air mix. But the two main types are **radiation or land fog**, and **advection or sea fog**.

Land fog occurs, generally in autumn and winter, when any warmth in the land is rapidly radiated into a clear sky so that the surface air is cooled below its dew point. A light breeze may help to diffuse the cooling effect and spread the fog – hence its importance to yachtsmen. It may drift out to sea for a few miles, particularly at dawn, when it is most prevalent.

Sea fog may also arrive from landward in the sense that warm air heated, for example, over the Continent, may release fog when it starts to move across the cool water of the North Sea. Fog in the Channel, especially in spring and early summer, may be brought by a warm, moist, south-westerly air stream blowing from the Azores across progressively colder seas. It is the critical rela-tionship of temperatures and humidity that matters and, unfortunately for sailors, once the potential for fog exists, a rising wind may not blow it away. Sea fog can persist in force 5 or even 6. The right tactics for dealing with it (discussed later) are vital.

'According to the wind indicator, it's easing.'

The Beaufort wind scale

Admiral Francis Beaufort's Scale of Wind Forces – what today we simply call the Beaufort scale – was originally defined in terms of the amount of sail a square rigged naval frigate could carry. Later it related to fishing smacks. Now the scale is used both on land and sea, with various ways of describing the effect of specified wind speeds.

Experienced sailors today relate the wind force they hear about in a forecast to the effect it has on the boat or boats they are familiar with – just like Admiral Beaufort did. When left to make their own assessments, most people begin by exaggerating wind forces, but then the written descriptions are not necessarily that much help. We have included them here anyway – as seen on land as well as at sea – in case you find them of some use, perhaps while driving down to the boat and listening to the forecast on the radio.

Warm front

Beaufort scale

Force	Wind speed in knots	Forecast description	Wave height in metres	Sea state	Effects on land
0	<1	Calm	0	Like a mirror	Smoke rises vertically
1	1–3	Light	0	Ripples without crests	Smoke, but not vanes, indicate wind direction
2	4–6	Light	0.1	Small wavelets, but crests do not break	Leaves rustle; wind vanes move
3	7–10	Light	0.4	Large wavelets; crests begin to break	Wind extends light flag
4	11–16	Moderate	1	Small waves; fairly frequent white horses	Wind raises dust and loose paper; small branches move
5	17–21	Fresh	2	Moderate, longer waves; many white horses	Small trees in leaf begin to sway
6	22–27	Strong breeze	3	Large waves with foam crests; spray likely	Telegraph wires whistle; umbrellas difficult to use
7	28–33	Near gale	4	Foam streaks begin to appear	Whole trees in motion
8	34–40	Gale	5.5	Longer waves, well marked with foam streaks	Twigs break off; walking is difficult
9	41–47	Severe gale	7	High waves with dense streaks of foam, spray and tumbling crests	Slight structural damage, eg to chimney pots and slates
10	48–55	Storm	9	Very high waves with long overhanging crests and large patches of foam; tumbling crests are heavy; visibility is affected	Trees uprooted; considerable structural damage

Sources of weather information

Nearly all weather forecasts originate from the **Meteorological Office** at Exeter. The forecast office can be consulted directly – by telephone (**Metcall**), fax (**Metfax**)   or internet (www.metoffice.gov.uk/shipping_forecast). But yachtsmen usually rely on a variety of indirect sources, some of which are accessible from an internet-capable mobile – **BBC shipping forecasts**, **local radio broadcasts**, the **Marinecall** telephone service, **Navtex** (for which a special receiver is needed), **Coastguard** inshore forecasts, **television** and **newspapers**.

Television forecasts, for example, are an excellent way to get a general picture of the weather before setting sail, often looking several days ahead. The BBC's presentation is especially thorough, using some of the professional terminology and often including satellite pictures in which swirling clouds delineate the moving weather fronts.

For coastal cruising, many yachtsmen find the Coastguard's four-hourly inshore waters forecasts on VHF radio particularly helpful. Crossing to the Continent, you will find many of these services replicated by the French Meteo, the German Wetterdienst and its Dutch equivalent (broadcasting in English as well as Dutch). A nautical almanac will give details.

Once at sea, within range of Radio 4, your main source is likely to be the BBC shipping forecast, a long-established maritime ritual conducted in concise, coded language and an unchanging sequence. There is no RYA requirement to draw your own weather map, but if you want have a go, this is your source. Using one of the RYA/Met Soc 'Metmaps' will make it a lot easier.

The shipping forecast

The Met Office prepares the shipping forecast four times a day for broadcast by BBC Radio 4 – currently on LW at 0048, 0520, 1201 and 1754. The first two of these broadcasts are followed by a supplementary forecast for the inshore waters of the UK, divided into nine areas.

The main shipping forecast consists of four elements:

- **Gale warnings** – a summary of any warnings in force.
- **A general synopsis**.
- **Area forecasts**.
- **Reports from coastal stations** (0048 and 0520 only).

Direction of buoyage

The **synopsis** gives the position of the main depressions, anticyclones, troughs and fronts from the latest analysis by the central forecast office (that is, about 6 hours previously), the central pressure of the lows and highs, and their expected movement over the next 24 hours – a deep low off southern Ireland, for example, might be expected to reach the North Sea by the same time on the following day.

The sea **area forecasts** come next, always in the same order, starting with Viking, off Norway, then clockwise round the British Isles through Humber and Thames, Wight and Portland, Rockall and Malin, to finish in South-East Iceland. (Sea area FitzRoy, incidentally, was recently re-named after the Victorian naval captain who devised the first weather forecasts.) For each area, details are given of changing wind, weather and visibility for the next 24 hours.

The five-minute bulletin ends twice a day with **reports from coastal stations** in a similar clockwise sequence – currently Tiree, Stornaway, Lerwick, Leuchars, Bridlington, Sandettie light vessel, Greenwich light vessel, Jersey, Channel light vessel, Scilly, Valentia, Ronaldsway and Malin Head – describing the local wind

'Did you catch the forecast?'

direction and force, the weather, the visibility in miles or metres, the atmospheric pressure in millibars, and how it is changing. Some of these weather stations, including the light vessels, are entirely automatic, with clever equipment for deducing from the local atmosphere how far a human being could see, as well as measuring wind and pressure.

The language of these forecasts is precise and economical. It forms a mesmeric pattern – fascinating even to non-sailors who have not the slightest practical interest in whether it is blowing a north-westerly gale on the Dogger Bank! Superfluous words like 'wind force' and 'visibility' are omitted, while each of those included has a careful definition. **Gale warnings** will be given if mean wind speeds of force 8 (34–40 knots) or gusts of more than 43 knots are expected; a gale is 'imminent' if it arrives within 6 hours; 'moderate' visibility is 2–5 miles.

When giving the forecast for sea area Dover, for example, the BBC announcer might simply say: 'Northwesterly 5, Fair, Good', meaning that the wind will blow from the north-west at force 5 (17–21 knots), the weather will be fair (that is, no rain showers, mist or fog), and the visibility good (more than 5 miles). The definitions may seem arbitrary, but they should be learned thoroughly, both to understand the forecast – and because they may be the subject of specific questions in the meteorology assessment paper.

'Its definitely thickening.'

Position of fog signal

Terminology in shipping forecasts

Gale warnings and timing
- **Gales** – mean wind speeds of F8 (34–40 knots) or gusts of more than 43 knots.
- **Severe gales** – mean wind speed of F9 (41–47 knots) or gusts of more than 51 knots.
- **Storm** – mean wind speed of F10 (48–55 knots) or gusts of more than 60 knots.
- **Imminent** – within 6 hours.
- **Soon** – in 6 to 12 hours.
- **Later** – in more than 12 hours.

Movement of pressure systems
- **Slowly** – up to 15 knots.
- **Steadily** – 15 to 25 knots.
- **Rather quickly** – 25 to 35 knots.
- **Rapidly** – 35 to 45 knots.
- **Very rapidly** – more than 45 knots.

Pressure tendency (change in previous three hours)
- **Steady** – less than 0.1 millibars.
- **Rising (or) falling slowly** – 0.1 to 1.5 millibars.
- **Rising (or) falling** – 1.6 to 3.5 millibars.

- **Rising (or) falling quickly** – 3.6 to 6.0 millibars.
- **Rising (or) falling very rapidly** – more than 6.0 millibars.
- **Now falling or now rising** – direction of change reversed.

Visibility
- **Good** – more than 5 nautical miles.
- **Moderate** – 2 to 5 nautical miles.
- **Poor** – 1000 metres to 2 nautical miles.
- **Fog** – less than 1000 metres.

To take all this information down and create your **own weather map** (an exercise that is not currently part of the Yachtmaster course) really requires the kind of forms and charts published by the RYA and the Met Office for this purpose, with the sequence of sea areas listed and marked. The charts may have scales for converting spacing of isobars into wind forces or knots (a cold front's pressure gradient produces relatively stronger winds than a warm one).

You will also need some sort of shorthand, however informal. Meteorologists have their own international plotting symbols, but there is also a simple **Beaufort notation**, using single letters which (apart from p for showers) are almost self-evident: **rain – r; drizzle – d; snow – s; showers – p; hail – h; thunder – t; squalls – q; mist – m; fog – f; haze – z; calm – o.** Wind directions and forces taken down as letters and numbers can be transferred to the chart with small half-feathered arrows .

But it matters little what symbols you use as long as they are intelligible and quick to record. The single letters L and H are obvious for low and high. A horizontal arrow can show that something – perhaps a wind direction and force – is 'becoming' something else; an oblique line will indicate the forecaster's habitual distinction between the situation 'at first' and 'later'. Coastal reports are easier to deal with than area forecasts because the pattern is clearly fixed, but you still have to move fast. Just the last two numbers will do for pressures. And in the last column, show the pressure tendency with a line – a horizontal one for 'steady', a sloping one for 'falling', and so on.

When you start drawing the isobars on the chart, do not expect them to produce the clear bold pattern found in textbook illustrations. Taken from a real shipping forecast, they can be maddeningly ambiguous.

Points to remember about the shipping forecast

- Concentrate on recording the essential elements of the general synopsis, even if you miss some of the area forecasts.
- If you get behind with the coastal reports, give priority to wind directions and pressures; these will help draw the first few isobars.
- Do not miss your own sea area while worrying about the others!

Starboard hand buoy

Safety and Seagoing Practice

The Rule of the Road

You don't need to be a sailor to know that ships carry a green navigation light on their starboard side and a red one to port, or that steam traditionally gives way to sail. Hire a motor cruiser on the Thames and the boatman will probably explain that in a narrow channel it is customary to 'drive on the right'.

Such basic principles were evolved as part of what maritime lawyers call 'the ordinary practice of seamen'. But nowadays they are codified, along with many more complex rules, in the *International Regulations for Preventing Collisions at Sea* – called the **colregs** for short. They are drafted by a London-based organisation known as the International Maritime Organisation (IMO), whose members include all the major maritime flag states.

The current regulations date from 1972, since when they have several times been amended. The fundamental principle of steam giving way to sail has survived, but only just. It is severely constrained by other rules that give priority to large commercial craft.

The regulations come in **four parts**:

A – general rules and definitions
B – steering and sailing rules
C – lights and shapes
D – sound and light signals

Most of these rules are of great practical importance at sea, whether you command a 5-ton yacht or a 50,000-ton tanker, and they form a correspondingly large part of the Yachtmaster course. We have therefore presented them almost in their entirety. But to make this large chunk digestible, we have included explanatory notes, occasional summaries, and a **variety of typefaces for different sorts of information**.

- The TEXT IN CAPITALS indicates KEY PHRASES, or in some cases complete rules, that may be worth skimming through just before the examination. Some of these are simply definitions; others are important because they convey in carefully drafted legal language some rule that would otherwise be ambiguous. The obligations of the 'stand-on' vessel in a crossing situation are a good example. Another rule of great significance to yachtsmen (because they have been heavily fined for disregarding it) states that vessels crossing traffic separation lanes shall do so 'as nearly as practicable at right angles to the general direction of traffic flow'. The essential text in capitals comprises about 1600 words, so it should take no more than 10–15 minutes to read right through.
- Less important sections of the rules are summarised here in square brackets – eg [rules apply in any visibility].
- *Text set in italic* denotes rules that are of *direct or special relevance to yachtsmen*. The steering rules for sailing vessels obviously come into this category – starboard tack has right of way, and so on – as do the navigation lights that must be carried by yachts.

- Explanatory notes and comments by the authors are tinted.

International Regulations for Preventing Collisions at Sea, 1972

Part A – General Rules and Definitions

Examiners can show a surprising predeliction for broad questions of definition, or tricky ones of the 'When is a door not a door?' variety! For that reason, this first section is worth more attention than you might otherwise give it.

Rule 1 – Application
a) These RULES shall APPLY TO ALL VESSELS UPON THE HIGH SEAS and in all waters connected therewith navigable by seagoing vessels.
b) Nothing in these rules shall interfere with the operation of special rules made by an appropriate authority for roadsteads, harbours, rivers, lakes or inland waterways . . .
c) [governments can make special rules for warships and fishing fleets]

'Beats me why they operate harbour signals for small boats like that.'

Rule 2 – Responsibility

a) Nothing in these rules shall exonerate any vessel or the owner, master or crew thereof, from the consequences of any neglect to comply with these rules or of the neglect of any precaution which may be required by the ordinary practice of seamen, or by the special circumstances of the case.

b) In construing and complying with these rules due regard shall be had to all dangers of navigation and collision and to any special circumstances, including the limitations of the vessels involved, which may make a departure from these rules necessary to avoid immediate danger.

> In other words, pedantic adherence to the written rules is not enough, either at sea or in the courtroom.

Rule 3 – General definitions

For the purpose of these rules, except where the context otherwise requires:

a) The word 'VESSEL' includes EVERY DESCRIPTION OF WATER CRAFT, including non-displacement craft and seaplanes . . .

b) The term 'POWER-DRIVEN VESSEL' means any vessel PROPELLED BY MACHINERY.

c) *The term 'SAILING VESSEL' means any vessel UNDER SAIL PROVIDED THAT PROPELLING MACHINERY, IF FITTED, IS NOT BEING USED.*

With her auxiliary engine switched on, a sailing yacht becomes a powerboat.

d) The term 'VESSEL ENGAGED IN FISHING' means any vessel fishing WITH NETS, LINES, TRAWLS OR OTHER FISHING APPARATUS WHICH RESTRICT MANOEUVRABILITY . . .

e) [definition of a seaplane]

f) The term 'VESSEL NOT UNDER COMMAND' means a vessel which THROUGH SOME EXCEPTIONAL CIRCUMSTANCES is UNABLE TO MANOEUVRE AS REQUIRED BY THESE RULES and is therefore unable to keep out of the way of another vessel.

g) The term 'RESTRICTED IN HER ABILITY TO MANOEUVRE' means a vessel which FROM THE NATURE OF HER WORK IS RESTRICTED in her ability to manoeuvre as required by these rules and is therefore unable to keep out of the way of another vessel. [there follows a series of examples of such vessels, including cable layers, dredgers, buoy tenders, survey ships, tugs engaged in towing, and warships minesweeping or launching aircraft]

h) The term 'VESSEL CONSTRAINED BY HER DRAFT' means a power-driven vessel which, because of her draught in relation to the available depth and width of navigable water, is SEVERELY RESTRICTED IN HER ABILITY TO DEVIATE from the course she is following.

i) The term 'UNDER WAY' means that a vessel is NOT AT ANCHOR, OR MADE FAST TO THE SHORE, OR AGROUND.

Note that 'under way' is not the same as 'making way through the water'.

j) [definition of dimensions]

k) Vessels shall be deemed to be in sight of one another only when one can be observed visually from the other.

Radar does not count as 'seeing'.

l) The term 'RESTRICTED VISIBILITY' means any conditions in which visibility is restricted by FOG, MIST, FALLING SNOW, HEAVY RAINSTORMS, SAND-STORMS or any other similar causes.

Transferred position line

PART B – Steering and Sailing Rules
Section 1 – Conduct of vessels in any condition of visibility

Some more definitions; a lot of good practical advice such as the need to make bold, early changes of course when avoiding collision; and the important Rule 10 on traffic separation schemes – its key message being that a small yacht must not 'impede the passage' of large commercial craft through such crowded waters.

Rule 4 – [rules apply in any visibility]

Rule 5 – Look-out

Every vessel shall at all times maintain a proper look-out by sight and hearing as well as by all available means appropriate in the prevailing circumstances and conditions so as to make a full appraisal of the situation and the risk of collision.

Fine sentiments, but remember they are no guarantee that a large ship will notice a small yacht under her bows.

Rule 6 – Safe speed

Every vessel shall at all times proceed at a safe speed so that she can take proper and effective action to avoid collision and be stopped within a distance appropriate to the prevailing circumstances and conditions.

In other words, in a seamanlike manner.

In determining a safe speed the following factors shall be among those taken into account:

a) By all vessels:
   (i)   the state of visibility
   (ii)   the traffic density including concentrations of fishing vessels . . .
   (iii)   the manoeuvrability of the vessel with special reference to stopping distance and turning ability . . .
   (iv)   at night the presence of background light such as from shore lights . . .
   (v)   the state of wind, sea and current, and the proximity of navigational hazards
   (vi)   the draught in relation to the available depth of water.

b) Additionally, by vessels with operational radar:
   (i)   the characteristics, efficiency and limitations of the radar equipment
          [five more sub-sections elaborating on (i)].

Rule 7 – Risk of collision

a) Every vessel shall use all available means appropriate to the prevailing circumstances and conditions to determine if risk of collision exists. If there is any doubt, such risk shall be deemed to exist.
b) Proper use shall be made of radar equipment if fitted and operational, including long-range scanning to obtain early warning of risk of collision and radar plotting or equivalent systematic observation of detected objects.

> To avoid the notorious 'radar-assisted' collision.

c) Assumptions shall not be made on the basis of scanty information, especially scanty radar information.
d) In determining if risk of collision exists, the following considerations shall be among those taken into account:
   (i)   SUCH RISK shall be deemed to exist IF THE COMPASS BEARING OF AN APPROACHING VESSEL DOES NOT APPRECIABLY CHANGE.

> A basic working rule, not just a legal precept.

   (ii)   such risk may sometimes exist even when an appreciable bearing change is evident, particularly when approaching a very large vessel, or a tow, or when approaching a vessel at close range.

Rule 8 – Action to avoid collision

a) Any ACTION TO AVOID COLLISION shall, if the circumstances of the case admit, be POSITIVE, made IN AMPLE TIME and with due regard to the observance of good seamanship.
b) ANY ALTERATION OF COURSE AND/OR SPEED to avoid collision shall, if the circumstances of the case permit, be LARGE ENOUGH TO BE READILY APPARENT TO ANOTHER VESSEL OBSERVING VISUALLY OR BY RADAR; a succession of small alterations of course and/or speed should be avoided.

> Points a) and b) offer excellent practical advice, especially when approaching large ships.

c) If there is sufficient sea room, alteration of course alone may be the most effective action to avoid a close-quarters situation provided that it is made in good time, is substantial, and does not result in another close-quarters situation.

Overfalls, tide rips, races

'Hold your course, John, we don't want to confuse him now.'

d) Action to avoid collision with another vessel shall be such as to result in passing at a safe distance . . .
e) If necessary to avoid collision or allow more time to assess the situation, a vessel shall slacken her speed or take all way off . . .
f) [this rule does not contradict rules about 'not impeding passage']

Rule 9 – Narrow channels

a) A VESSEL proceeding along the course of a narrow channel or fairway SHALL KEEP as near TO THE OUTER LIMIT OF THE CHANNEL OR FAIRWAY WHICH LIES ON HER STARBOARD SIDE as is safe and practicable.
b) *A vessel of less than 20 metres in length or a SAILING VESSEL SHALL NOT IMPEDE THE PASSAGE OF A VESSEL WHICH CAN SAFELY NAVIGATE ONLY WITHIN A NARROW CHANNEL or fairway.*
c) A VESSEL ENGAGED IN FISHING SHALL NOT IMPEDE THE PASSAGE of any other vessel navigating within a narrow channel or fairway.

d) A VESSEL SHALL NOT CROSS A NARROW CHANNEL OR FAIRWAY IF SUCH CROSSING IMPEDES the passage of a vessel which can safely navigate only within such channel or fairway. The latter vessel may use the sound signal prescribed in **Rule 34d**

(Five short and rapid blasts.)

if in doubt as to the intention of the crossing vessel.

e) (i)   In a narrow channel or fairway when overtaking can take place only if the vessel to be overtaken takes action to permit safe passing, the VESSEL INTENDING TO OVERTAKE shall indicate her intention by SOUNDING THE APPROPRIATE SIGNAL prescribed in **Rule 34c (i)**

(Two long blasts and one short blast if overtaking to starboard; two long and two short to port.)

The VESSEL TO BE OVERTAKEN shall, IF IN AGREEMENT, SOUND THE APPROPRIATE SIGNAL prescribed in **Rule 34c (ii)**

(Long, short, long, short blasts.)

and take steps to permit safe passing. IF IN DOUBT she MAY SOUND THE SIGNALS prescribed in **Rule 34d**

(Five short and rapid blasts.)

(ii)   [**Rule 13** still applies, ie keep clear when overtaking]

f) A VESSEL NEARING A BEND or an area of a narrow channel or fairway where other vessels may be obscured by an intervening obstruction shall navigate with particular alertness and caution and shall SOUND THE APPROPRIATE SIGNAL prescribed in **Rule 34e**

(One long blast.)

g) ANY VESSEL shall, if the circumstances of the case admit, AVOID ANCHORING IN A NARROW CHANNEL.

Rule 10 – Traffic separation schemes

a) This rule applies to traffic separation schemes adopted by IMO and does not relieve any vessel of her obligation under any other rule.

b) A VESSEL USING A TRAFFIC SCHEME shall:
   (i)   PROCEED in the appropriate traffic lane IN THE GENERAL DIRECTION OF TRAFFIC for that lane;

Isolated danger mark

(ii)   so far as practicable KEEP CLEAR OF a traffic separation line or SEPARATION ZONE;

(iii) NORMALLY JOIN OR LEAVE A TRAFFIC LANE AT THE TERMINATION of the lane . . .

c) A VESSEL SHALL so far as practicable avoid crossing traffic lanes, but if obliged to do so, shall CROSS ON A HEADING AS NEARLY AS PRACTICABLE AT RIGHT ANGLES TO THE GENERAL DIRECTION OF TRAFFIC FLOW.

> This is obviously a particularly important rule for yachts crossing the English Channel. Its purpose is to minimise the time spent in the traffic lanes by steering straight across instead of heading up-tide to make good a right-angled course. Coastguards watching on radar will, or should, allow for this. The phrase 'as nearly as practicable' also covers a yacht's inability to sail straight into the wind.

d) Inshore traffic zones shall not normally be used by through traffic which can safely use the appropriate traffic lane within the adjacent traffic separation scheme. However *VESSELS OF LESS THAN 20 METRES IN LENGTH AND SAILING VESSELS MAY UNDER ALL CIRCUMSTANCES USE INSHORE TRAFFIC ZONES.*

e) A VESSEL OTHER THAN A CROSSING VESSEL or a vessel joining or leaving a lane shall NOT NORMALLY ENTER A SEPARATION ZONE or cross a separation line EXCEPT: in case of EMERGENCY to avoid immediate danger; to engage in FISHING within a separation zone.

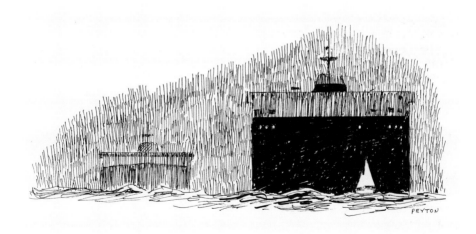

'I always play safe and go astern of them.'

f) [take care near the end of traffic schemes]
g) [avoid anchoring in or near schemes]
h) [give schemes a wide berth]
i) [fishing vessels must not impede vessels using schemes]
j) *A VESSEL OF LESS THAN 20 METRES OR A SAILING VESSEL shall NOT IMPEDE THE SAFE PASSAGE OF A POWER-DRIVEN VESSEL FOLLOWING A TRAFFIC LANE.*
k) [scheme maintenance vessels may be exempt from this rule]
l) [cable layers may be exempt from this rule]

Section 2 – Conduct of vessels in sight of one another

Rule 11 – *[this section covers vessels in sight of one another]*

Rule 12 – Sailing vessels

a) *When two sailing vessels are approaching one another so as to involve the risk of collision, one of them shall keep out of the way of the other as follows:*
   (i)   *when each has the WIND ON A DIFFERENT SIDE, the vessel which has the wind on the PORT SIDE SHALL KEEP OUT OF THE WAY of the other;*
   (ii)   *when both have the WIND ON THE SAME SIDE, the vessel which is to WINDWARD SHALL KEEP OUT OF THE WAY of the vessel which is to leeward;*
   (iii) *if a vessel with the wind on the port side sees a vessel to windward and CANNOT DETERMINE WITH CERTAINTY whether the other vessel has the wind on the port or the starboard side, she shall KEEP OUT OF THE WAY of the other.*
b) *For the purposes of this rule the WINDWARD SIDE shall be deemed to be the side OPPOSITE TO that on which the MAINSAIL is carried or, in the case of a square-rigged vessel, the side opposite to that on which the largest fore-and-aft sail is carried.*

Summary – starboard tack has right of way; on same tack, windward boat gives way; if in doubt, keep clear.

Rule 13 – Overtaking

a) Notwithstanding anything contained in the rules ANY VESSEL OVERTAKING any other shall KEEP OUT OF THE WAY of the vessel being overtaken.

Lighted offshore platform

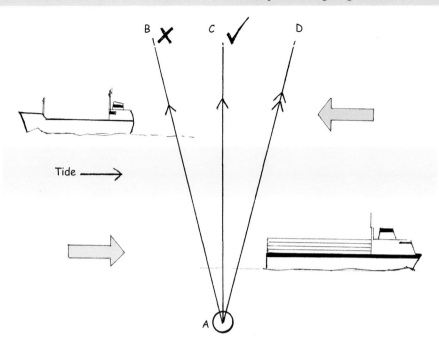

Crossing shipping lanes. Normally, to arrive at C, a yachtsman would steer course AB to allow for the tide. The correct procedure, however, is to steer AC and, because of the tidal set, arrive at D.

b) A vessel shall be deemed to be OVERTAKING WHEN coming up with another vessel FROM A DIRECTION MORE THAN 22.5° ABAFT HER BEAM, that is, in such a position with reference to the vessel she is overtaking that AT NIGHT she would be able to SEE ONLY THE STERNLIGHT of that vessel, but neither of her sidelights.

c) When a vessel is in doubt as to whether she is overtaking another, she shall assume that this is the case, and act accordingly.

Note the general principle, also applied in Rules 12 and 14, that if in doubt you keep clear.

d) Any subsequent alteration of the bearing between the two vessels shall not make the overtaking vessel a crossing vessel within the meaning of these rules, or relieve her of the duty of keeping clear of the overtaken vessel until she is finally past and clear.

The disastrous collision off the Isle of Wight in 1970 between the tankers *Pacific Glory* and *Allegro* involved the potential conflict – referred to here – between Rule 13 and the crossing rule, Rule 15.

Rule 14 – Head-on situation

a) When TWO POWER-DRIVEN VESSELS are MEETING ON RECIPROCAL OR NEARLY RECIPROCAL COURSES so as to involve the risk of collision EACH SHALL ALTER HER COURSE TO STARBOARD so that each shall pass on the port side of the other.
b) Such a situation shall be deemed to exist when a vessel sees the other ahead or nearly ahead and by night she can see the masthead lights of the other in line or nearly in line and/or both sidelights, and by day she observes the corresponding aspect of the other vessel.
c) When a vessel is in any doubt as to whether such a situation exists, she shall assume that it does and act accordingly.

Generations of sailors have learnt this rule by memorising Thomas Gray's verses:

When you see three lights ahead,
Starboard wheel and show your Red,
Green to Green or Red to Red,
Perfect safety, go ahead.

Rule 15 – Crossing situation

When TWO POWER-DRIVEN VESSELS are CROSSING so as to involve risk of collision, the VESSEL WHICH HAS THE OTHER ON HER OWN STARBOARD SIDE SHALL KEEP OUT OF THE WAY and shall, if the circumstances of the case admit, avoid crossing ahead of the other vessel.

The Thomas Gray version goes like this:

If to your starboard Red appear,
It is your duty to keep clear,
But when upon your port is seen
A steamer's starboard light of Green,
There's not so much for you to do;
The green light must keep clear of you.

Wreck: not dangerous

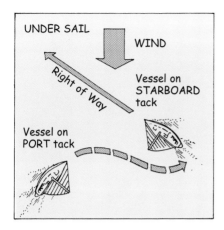

UNDER SAIL

WIND

Right of Way

Vessel on STARBOARD tack

Vessel on PORT tack

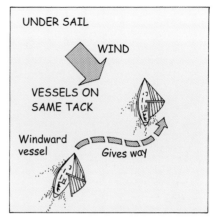

UNDER SAIL

WIND

VESSELS ON SAME TACK

Windward vessel

Gives way

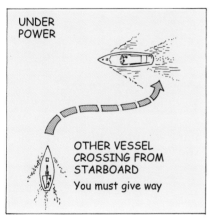

UNDER POWER

OTHER VESSEL CROSSING FROM STARBOARD

You must give way

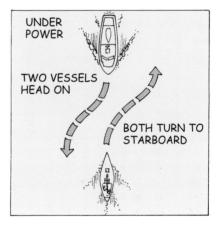

UNDER POWER

TWO VESSELS HEAD ON

BOTH TURN TO STARBOARD

'I'll be glad to get in, I've had enough excitement for one day.'

Rule 16 – Action by give-way vessel

Every vessel which is directed to keep out of the way of another vessel shall, so far as possible, take early and substantial action to keep well clear.

> Note the 'early and substantial'

Rule 17 – Action by stand-on-vessel

a) (i)   WHERE ONE of two vessels IS TO KEEP OUT OF THE WAY, THE OTHER SHALL KEEP HER COURSE AND SPEED.

   (ii)   The LATTER MAY HOWEVER TAKE ACTION to avoid collision BY HER MANOEUVRE ALONE AS SOON AS it becomes apparent to her that the VESSEL REQUIRED TO KEEP OUT OF THE WAY IS NOT TAKING APPROPRIATE ACTION in compliance with these rules.

b) When, from any cause, the vessel required to keep her course and speed finds herself so close that collision cannot be avoided by the action of the give-way vessel alone, she shall take such action as will best aid to avoid collision.

I require assistance

The careful legal wording of a) and b), though perhaps confusing, is vital in some collision situations between large vessels. Small yachts should try to apply the more basic rules of self-preservation.

c) A POWER-DRIVEN VESSEL WHICH TAKES ACTION IN A CROSSING SITUATION in accordance with sub-paragraph a) (ii) of this rule to avoid collision with another power-driven vessel SHALL, if the circumstances of the case permit, NOT ALTER COURSE TO PORT FOR A VESSEL ON HER OWN PORT SIDE.
d) This rule does not relieve the give-way vessel of her obligation to keep out of the way.

Rule 18 – Responsibilities between vessels

The following marine hierarchy, or 'pecking order', is obvious exam material, and worth learning. Once again, remember that an auxiliary sailing yacht is a 'power-driven vessel' when her engine is being used.

Except where **Rules 9, 10** and 13 otherwise require –
a) A POWER-DRIVEN VESSEL under way shall KEEP OUT OF THE WAY OF:
   (i)   A VESSEL NOT UNDER COMMAND;
   (ii)   A VESSEL RESTRICTED IN HER ABILITY TO MANOEUVRE;
   (iii) A VESSEL ENGAGED IN FISHING;
   (iv) A SAILING VESSEL.
b) *A SAILING VESSEL under way shall keep out of the way of:*
   (i)   A VESSEL NOT UNDER COMMAND;
   (ii)   A VESSEL RESTRICTED IN HER ABILITY TO MANOEUVRE;
   (iii) A VESSEL ENGAGED IN FISHING.
c) A VESSEL ENGAGED IN FISHING when under way shall, so far as possible, keep out of the way of:
   (i)   A VESSEL NOT UNDER COMMAND;
   (ii)   A VESSEL RESTRICTED IN HER ABILITY TO MANOEUVRE.
d) (i)   ANY VESSEL OTHER THAN A VESSEL NOT UNDER COMMAND OR A VESSEL RESTRICTED IN HER ABILITY TO MANOEUVRE shall, if the circumstances of the case admit, AVOID IMPEDING THE SAFE PASSAGE of a VESSEL CONSTRAINED BY HER DRAUGHT, exhibiting the signals in **Rule 28**

Three vertical all-round reds or a cylinder.

   (ii)   [a vessel constrained by her draught should take special care]
e) [seaplanes should keep well clear]

The maritime 'pecking order'

Vessel Not Under Command
Vessel Restricted in her Ability to Manoeuvre
Vessel Constrained by her Draught
Fishing Vessel – provided she is actually engaged in fishing
Sailing Vessel – but she loses this status when using an auxiliary engine
Power-driven Vessel – she gains status when following a traffic separation lane
Seaplane – definitely bottom of the pile

Modern commercial ships are often big, clumsy and fast. They can be upon you from over the horizon in less than 10 minutes; they may need 5 or 6 miles to stop; they can rarely take quick avoiding action. In reality, therefore, the seafaring status of a small sailing yacht is less than the colregs would suggest. She should stay clear of her big sisters whenever possible, especially in crowded waters and harbour entrances, and she should definitely not rely on the tradition of steam giving way to sail.

Section 3 – Conduct of vessels in restricted visibility

This is a section of the rules not always fully observed, and one where the relatively privileged legal position still enjoyed by small sailing craft is more than usually artificial.

Rule 19

a) [applies to vessels that cannot see one another]
b) EVERY VESSEL SHALL PROCEED AT A SAFE SPEED ADAPTED TO THE PREVAILING CIRCUMSTANCES and conditions of restricted visibility. A power-driven vessel shall have her engines ready for immediate manoeuvre.
c) [take account of poor visibility when following other rules]
d) A vessel which detects by radar alone the presence of another vessel shall determine if a close-quarters situation is developing and/or risk of collision exists. If so, she shall take avoiding action in ample time, provided that when such action consists of an alteration of course, so far as possible the following shall be avoided:

West cardinal buoy

(i) an alteration of course to port for a vessel forward of the beam, other than for a vessel being overtaken;

(ii) an alteration of course towards a vessel abeam or abaft the beam.

e) Except where it has been determined that a risk of collision does not exist, every vessel which hears apparently forward of her beam the fog signal of another vessel, or which cannot avoid a close-quarters situation with another vessel forward of her beam, shall reduce her speed to the minimum at which she can be kept on her course. She shall if necessary take all her way off and in any event navigate with extreme caution until danger of collision is over.

PART C – Lights and shapes

Laid out merely as a mass of overlapping regulations, the rules on lights and shapes can look dreadfully confusing. But by logical grouping and elimination – which we have tried to apply in the illustrations – they can be made more manageable. After all, every one of them, from the multi-coloured array that makes a dredger look like a floating Christmas tree, to a small sailing boat's solitary white light, is designed to convey information.

Of the four colours in the basic rules, one can quickly be disposed of because it so rarely occurs. A steady yellow light is confined to tugs, shown above the sternlight to indicate that the vessel is towing. A hover-craft has a flashing yellow light, and a vessel fishing with a seine net may show a pair of alternately flashing yellow lights if she is hampered by her gear. Apart from these few cases – and the lifeboat's blue flashing light – we are dealing with combinations of white, red and green.

The first distinction to be made here is between directional lights that are meant to convey a perspective of movement through the darkness, and all-round lights which generally tell you what sort of vessel you are looking at. A large ship's basic navigation lights, for example, consist of red and green sidelights and a pair of forward-facing white masthead lights, with the rear one set higher than the other so you can tell instantly which way she is heading. But the additional green and white lights shown by a fishing trawler – whether or not she is moving – are visible all round. So are the white and red lights carried by a pilot vessel (same colours as the pilot flag H) or the two reds of a vessel not under command.

The colour red, you will notice, is generally associated with situations of difficulty or danger – vessels aground, manoeuvring with difficulty, constrained by their draught, and so on.

Another principle running through the IMO system is that you add lights as the vessel – or combination of vessels – gets larger. A small tug on her own may show just a single masthead light, for instance. A tug more than 50 metres long must carry a second, similar light aft. When towing, the forward light is doubled up, and if the length of the tow exceeds 200 metres, she adds a third. Seen from dead ahead, therefore, she will by now present a vertical line of four white lights, plus the red and green sidelights to port and starboard.

Rule 21 – Definitions

a) 'MASTHEAD LIGHT' – [white light over arc of 225° FROM RIGHT AHEAD TO 22.5° ABAFT THE BEAM on each side]
b) 'SIDELIGHTS' – [red to port, green to starboard, in each case over ARC OF 112.5° FROM RIGHT AHEAD TO 22.5° ABAFT THE BEAM; but in *VESSEL LESS THAN 20 METRES LONG SIDELIGHTS MAY BE COMBINED IN ONE LANTERN on centreline*]
c) 'STERNLIGHT' – [CENTRED AFT TO SHOW OVER ARC OF 135° NOT COVERED BY MASTHEAD AND SIDELIGHTS]
d) 'Towing light' – [same as sternlight but yellow]

Rule 22 – Visibility of lights

a) Vessels of 50 metres or more in length: masthead 6 miles; others 3 miles.
b) Vessels of 12–50 metres: masthead 5 miles (3 miles if less than 20 metres long); others 2 miles.
c) *Vessels of less than 12 metres: masthead/sternlight/towing light/all-round light 2 miles; sidelight 1 mile.*

Rule 23 – Power-driven vessels under way

a) A POWER-DRIVEN VESSEL UNDER WAY shall exhibit:
    (i)   a MASTHEAD LIGHT forward;
    (ii)   a SECOND MASTHEAD LIGHT abaft of and higher than the forward one *(except that a VESSEL OF LESS THAN 50 METRES in length SHALL NOT BE OBLIGED TO exhibit such light, but may do so)*;
    (iii)   SIDELIGHTS;
    (iv)   a STERNLIGHT.
b) An AIR-CUSHION VESSEL when operating in the non-displacement mode shall, in addition to the lights prescribed in paragraph a) of this rule, exhibit an ALL-ROUND FLASHING LIGHT.
c) (i)   *A POWER-DRIVEN VESSEL OF LESS THAN 12 METRES in length may in lieu of the lights prescribed in paragraph a) of this rule exhibit an ALL-ROUND WHITE LIGHT AND SIDELIGHTS.*

Fog

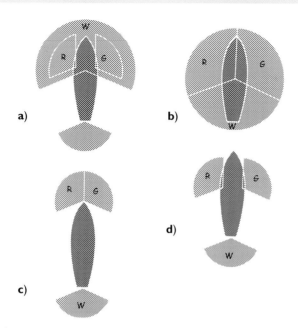

All vessels are required to carry navigation lights between sunset and sunrise apart from very small boats which are only required to carry a torch. In the diagrams R = red, W = white and G = green; a) power-driven vessels, including those with sails and auxiliary engine, carry sidelights, a masthead light and sternlight; b) a sailing vessel of less than 20 metres may carry a tricolour light high on the mast (in place of sidelights and stern-light) c) a sailing boat less than 20 metres may carry a bicolour light and sternlight or d) sidelights and sternlight.

(ii)   *A POWER-DRIVEN VESSEL OF LESS THAN 7 METRES in length whose maximum speed does not exceed 7 knots may in lieu of the lights pre scribed in paragraph a) of this rule exhibit an ALL-ROUND WHITE LIGHT and shall, if practicable, also exhibit sidelights.*

Rule 24 – Towing and pushing

a) A POWER-DRIVEN VESSEL WHEN TOWING shall exhibit:
(i)   instead of the light prescribed in **Rule 23a (i)**

The forward masthead light,

TWO MASTHEAD LIGHTS FORWARD in a vertical line; WHEN THE LENGTH OF THE TOW, measuring from the stern of the towing vessel to the after end of the tow, EXCEEDS 200 METRES, THREE SUCH LIGHTS in a vertical line;

9

    (ii)   SIDELIGHTS;

    (iii)   a STERNLIGHT;

    (iv)   a TOWING LIGHT in a vertical line ABOVE THE STERNLIGHT;

    (v)   WHEN THE LENGTH OF THE TOW EXCEEDS 200 METRES, A DIAMOND SHAPE (by day) where it can best be seen.

> In other words, the characteristics of a tug towing at night are the extra white masthead lights when seen from ahead and, usually, the yellow towing light seen from astern.

b) When a pushing vessel and a vessel being pushed ahead are rigidly connected in a composite unit they shall be regarded as a power-driven vessel and exhibit the lights prescribed in **Rule 23**.

c) A POWER-DRIVEN VESSEL WHEN PUSHING AHEAD OR TOWING ALONGSIDE, except in the case of a composite unit, shall exhibit:

    (i)   instead of the light prescribed in **Rule 23a (i)**

> (the forward masthead light),

    TWO MASTHEAD LIGHTS FORWARD in a vertical line;

    (ii)   SIDELIGHTS;

    (iii)   a STERNLIGHT.

> Note the absence of the yellow towing light in this situation.

d) A power-driven vessel to which paragraphs a) or c) of this rule apply shall also comply with **Rule 23a (ii)**.

> Covering the second masthead light aft in larger vessels.

e) A VESSEL OR OBJECT BEING TOWED, other than those mentioned in paragraph g) of the rule

> (ie semi-submerged),

shall exhibit:

    (i)   SIDELIGHTS;

    (ii)   a STERNLIGHT;

    (iii)   when the length of the tow exceeds 200 metres, a diamond shape where it can best be seen.

f) Provided that any number of vessels being towed alongside or pushed in a group shall be lighted as one vessel: a vessel being pushed ahead, not being part of a composite unit, shall exhibit at the forward end, sidelights; a vessel being towed alongside shall exhibit a sternlight and at the forward end, sidelights.

g) An inconspicuous partly submerged vessel or object, or combination of such vessels or objects being towed, shall exhibit... [multiple all-round white lights and diamonds to indicate their size].

h) Where from any sufficient cause it is impracticable for a vessel or object being towed to exhibit the lights or shapes prescribed in paragraphs e) or g) of this rule, all possible measures shall be taken to light the vessel or object towed or at least to indicate its presence

(eg using a searchlight to illuminate the tow).

Rule 25 – Sailing vessels under way and vessels under oars

a) *A SAILING VESSEL UNDER WAY shall exhibit:*
   (i)   *SIDELIGHTS;*
   (ii) *a STERNLIGHT;*
b) *In a SAILING VESSEL OF LESS THAN 20 METRES in length the LIGHTS pre-scribed in paragraph a) of this rule MAY BE COMBINED IN ONE LANTERN carried at or near the top of the mast where it can best be seen.*
c) *A SAILING VESSEL under way may, IN ADDITION to the lights prescribed in paragraph a) of this rule, exhibit at or near the top of the mast, where they can best be seen, TWO ALL-ROUND LIGHTS in a vertical line, THE UPPER BEING RED AND THE LOWER GREEN, but these lights shall not be exhibited in conjunction with the combined lantern permitted by paragraph b) of this rule.*
d) *A SAILING VESSEL OF LESS THAN 7 METRES in length shall, if practicable, exhibit the lights prescribed in paragraph a) or b) of this rule, but if she does not, she shall have ready at hand AN ELECTRIC TORCH OR LIGHTED LANTERN showing a white light which shall be exhibited in sufficient time to prevent collision. A VESSEL UNDER OARS may exhibit the lights pre-scribed in this rule for sailing vessels, but if she does not, she shall have ready at hand AN ELECTRIC TORCH OR LIGHTED LANTERN showing a white light which shall be exhibited in sufficient time to prevent collision.*
e) *A VESSEL PROCEEDING UNDER SAIL (in daylight) WHEN ALSO BEING PROPELLED BY MACHINERY shall exhibit forward where it can best be seen A CONICAL SHAPE DOWNWARDS.*

This is rarely observed.

Rule 26 – Fishing vessels

a) A vessel engaged in fishing, whether under way or at anchor, shall exhibit only the lights and shapes prescribed in this rule.

Wishful thinking!

b) A VESSEL ENGAGED IN TRAWLING . . . shall exhibit:
  (i)   TWO ALL-ROUND LIGHTS in a vertical line, THE UPPER BEING GREEN AND THE OTHER WHITE, or (by day) a shape consisting of two cones with their apexes together in a vertical line one above the other;
  (ii)   A MASTHEAD LIGHT ABAFT OF AND HIGHER THAN THE ALL-ROUND GREEN LIGHT; a vessel of less than 50 metres in length shall not be obliged to exhibit such a light but may do so;
  (iii) when making way through the water, in addition to the lights prescribed in this paragraph, SIDELIGHTS and a STERNLIGHT.

Note that the single green all-round light is characteristic only of the trawler, although a dredger and a minesweeper may show two or three green lights respectively.

c) A VESSEL ENGAGED IN FISHING OTHER THAN TRAWLING shall exhibit:
  (i)   TWO ALL-ROUND LIGHTS in a vertical line, THE UPPER BEING RED AND THE LOWER WHITE, or (by day) a shape consisting of two cones with apexes together in a line one above the other;
  (ii)   when there is OUTLYING GEAR extending more than 150 metres horizontally from the vessel, an ALL-ROUND WHITE LIGHT OR A CONE APEX UPWARDS IN THE DIRECTION OF THE GEAR;
  (iii) WHEN MAKING WAY THROUGH THE WATER . . . SIDELIGHTS and a STERNLIGHT.
  [Annex II prescribes extra light signals for trawlers: TWO VERTICAL WHITE LIGHTS when SHOOTING their nets, WHITE OVER RED when HAULING nets, and TWO VERTICAL REDS when NETS FAST on an obstruction; TRAWLERS FISHING IN PAIRS may direct SEARCHLIGHTS at each other. The Annex also prescribes signals for purse seiners: TWO VERTICAL YELLOW LIGHTS, FLASH-ING ALTERNATELY every second, but only when the vessel is hampered by her gear].

Rule 27 – Vessels not under command or restricted in their ability to manoeuvre

a) A VESSEL NOT UNDER COMMAND

(NUC for short)

shall exhibit:

Dangerous underwater wreck

(i)   TWO ALL-ROUND RED LIGHTS in a vertical line where they can best be seen;

(ii)   TWO BALLS (by day) or similar shapes in a vertical line where they can best be seen;

(iii) WHEN MAKING WAY through the water . . . SIDELIGHTS and a STERN LIGHT [in addition to two reds].

b) A VESSEL RESTRICTED IN HER ABILITY TO MANOEUVRE

(known as RAM),

except a vessel engaged in mine clearance operations, shall exhibit:

(i)   THREE ALL-ROUND LIGHTS in a vertical line where they can best be seen; the HIGHEST AND LOWEST of these lights shall be RED and the MIDDLE light shall be WHITE;

(ii)   THREE SHAPES

(by day)

in a vertical line where they can best be seen; the HIGHEST AND LOWEST of these shapes shall be BALLS and the MIDDLE one a DIAMOND;

(iii) WHEN MAKING WAY through the water, a MASTHEAD LIGHT or LIGHTS, SIDELIGHTS and a STERNLIGHT [in addition to three red/white/red];

(iv) when AT ANCHOR [in addition to red/white/red and shapes] the lights or shape prescribed in **Rule 30**

(ie at least one all-round white light forward, or one ball).

c) [A power-driven vessel hampered by towing should show a tug's lights and those of a vessel restricted in her ability to manoeuvre]

d) A VESSEL ENGAGED IN DREDGING or underwater operations, when restricted in her ability to manoeuvre, shall exhibit the lights and shapes prescribed in this rule and, in addition, when an obstruction exists:

(i)   TWO ALL-ROUND RED LIGHTS OR TWO BALLS in a vertical line TO INDICATE the side on which the OBSTRUCTION exists;

(ii)   TWO ALL-ROUND GREEN LIGHTS OR TWO DIAMONDS in a vertical line TO INDICATE the side on which another VESSEL MAY PASS;

(iii) [at anchor this rule still applies, not **Rule 30**]

e) Whenever the size of a VESSEL ENGAGED IN DIVING OPERATIONS makes it impracticable to exhibit all lights and shapes prescribed in this rule, the following shall be exhibited:

(i)   THREE ALL-ROUND LIGHTS in a vertical line where they can best be seen; the HIGHEST AND LOWEST of these lights shall be RED and the MIDDLE light shall be WHITE;

'Coastguard on the radio wanting the name and address of your next of kin.'

(ii)   a rigid replica of the INTERNATIONAL CODE FLAG 'A' not less than one metre in height.

f) A VESSEL ENGAGED IN MINE CLEARANCE OPERATIONS shall, in addition to the lights prescribed in Rules 23 and 30, exhibit THREE ALL-ROUND GREEN LIGHTS OR THREE BALLS; one of these lights or shapes shall be exhibited near the foremast head and one at each end of the fore yard. These lights or shapes indicate that it is DANGEROUS for another vessel TO APPROACH WITHIN 1000 METRES of the mine clearance vessel.

g) [vessels of less than 12 metres need not comply with this rule unless engaged in diving operations]

Rule 28 – Vessels constrained by their draught

A VESSEL CONSTRAINED BY HER DRAUGHT

CBD for short

may, in addition to the lights prescribed for power-driven vessels in Rule 23, exhibit where they can best be seen THREE ALL-ROUND RED LIGHTS in a vertical line OR A CYLINDER.

Visitors' moorings

Signalling the Pecking Order

NUC	two vertical reds or two balls
RAM	three vertical red/white/red or ball/diamond/ball
CBD	three vertical reds or a cylinder
Fishing	green over white or red over white, or twin cones
Sailing	red over green or combined red and green
Power	white all-round or masthead white

Rule 29 – Pilot vessels

a) A VESSEL ENGAGED ON PILOTAGE DUTY shall exhibit:
- (i) at or near the masthead, TWO ALL-ROUND LIGHTS in a vertical line, the UPPER BEING WHITE AND THE LOWER RED;
- (ii) WHEN UNDER WAY, in addition, SIDELIGHTS AND A STERNLIGHT;
- (iii) when at anchor, in addition to the lights prescribed in this rule, the lights or shape prescribed in **Rule 30** for vessels at anchor.

Rule 30 – Anchored vessels and vessels aground

a) A VESSEL AT ANCHOR shall exhibit where it can best be seen:
- (i) IN THE FORE PART, an ALL-ROUND WHITE LIGHT OR ONE BALL;
- (ii) at or NEAR THE STERN AND AT A LOWER LEVEL than the light prescribed in sub-paragraph (i), an ALL-ROUND WHITE LIGHT.

b) A VESSEL OF LESS THAN 50 METRES in length may exhibit an ALL-ROUND WHITE LIGHT WHERE IT CAN BEST BE SEEN instead of the lights prescribed in paragraph a) of this rule.

c) A vessel at anchor may, and A VESSEL OF 100 METRES AND MORE in length SHALL, ALSO USE THE AVAILABLE WORKING OR EQUIVALENT LIGHTS to illuminate her decks.

d) A VESSEL AGROUND shall exhibit the lights prescribed in paragraph a) or b) of this rule and IN ADDITION, where they can best be seen:
- (i) TWO ALL-ROUND RED LIGHTS in a vertical line;
- (ii) THREE BALLS in a vertical line.

e) *A VESSEL OF LESS THAN 7 METRES in length, when AT ANCHOR NOT IN OR NEAR A NARROW CHANNEL, FAIRWAY OR ANCHORAGE, or where other vessels normally navigate, SHALL NOT BE REQUIRED [to comply with this rule].*

f) *A VESSEL OF LESS THAN 12 METRES in length, WHEN AGROUND SHALL NOT BE REQUIRED [to comply with this rule].*

2 vertical red lights

In spite of the immense care taken in drafting the colregs, the lights prescribed in Rules 20 to 30 can occasionally be ambiguous, and when at sea they can often be confusing.

To take the simplest example – a single white light: for exam purposes it could be several things (sternlight, anchor light, small powerboat under way); at sea, the context might resolve the ambiguity (a power boat will move, whereas an anchor light will not); but if the observer is also confronted by an array of shorelights, the single white might simply go unnoticed.

Because the surrounding darkness deprives you of other references, distant shore lights can temporarily be mistaken for a mysterious – non-existent – vessel close to. And certain types of ship are notoriously confusing – warships, fishing vessels, ferries, or any other vessel whose decks are ablaze with working lights. By contrast, the twin masthead lights and sidelights of a darkened ship are remarkably effective in conveying her relative movement.

PART D – Sound and light signals

Rule 32 – Definitions

b) ['short blast' means about 1 second]
c) ['prolonged blast' means 4–6 seconds]

Rule 33 – Equipment for sound signals

a) A VESSEL OF 12 METRES OR MORE in length shall be provided with a WHISTLE AND A BELL, and a VESSEL OF 100 METRES OR MORE in length shall, IN ADDITION, be provided with a GONG, the tone and sound of which cannot be confused with that of the bell.

b) *A VESSEL OF LESS THAN 12 METRES in length shall NOT be OBLIGED TO CARRY the SOUND SIGNALLING APPLIANCES PRESCRIBED in this rule, but IF SHE DOES NOT, she shall be provided with SOME OTHER MEANS of making an efficient sound signal.*

Rule 34 – Manoeuvring and warning signals

a) When vessels are in sight of one another, a POWER-DRIVEN VESSEL UNDER WAY, when manoeuvring as authorised or required by these rules, shall indicate that manoeuvre by the following signals on her whistle: ONE SHORT BLAST – 'I AM ALTERING MY COURSE TO STARBOARD'
TWO SHORT BLASTS – 'I AM ALTERING MY COURSE TO PORT'
THREE SHORT BLASTS – 'I AM OPERATING ASTERN PROPULSION'

Vessel not under command

b) ANY VESSEL MAY SUPPLEMENT the WHISTLE SIGNALS prescribed in this rule BY LIGHT SIGNALS:
ONE FLASH – 'I AM ALTERING MY COURSE TO STARBOARD'
TWO FLASHES – 'I AM ALTERING MY COURSE TO PORT'
THREE FLASHES – 'I AM OPERATING ASTERN PROPULSION'
[ie 1-second flashes, and 10 seconds between signals; signalling light is white, all-round, visible at minimum of 5 miles]

c) When in sight of one another in a narrow channel or fairway:
   (i)   a VESSEL INTENDING TO OVERTAKE another shall in compliance with **Rule 9e (i)** indicate her intention by the following signals on her whistle:
TWO PROLONGED BLASTS FOLLOWED BY ONE SHORT – 'I INTEND TO OVERTAKE YOU ON YOUR STARBOARD SIDE'
TWO PROLONGED BLASTS FOLLOWED BY TWO SHORT – 'I INTEND TO OVERTAKE YOU ON YOUR PORT SIDE'
   (ii)   the VESSEL ABOUT TO BE OVERTAKEN when acting in accordance with **Rule 9e (i)**
shall INDICATE AGREEMENT by the following signal on her whistle:
ONE PROLONGED, ONE SHORT, ONE PROLONGED AND ONE SHORT BLAST

d) When vessels in sight of one another are approaching each other and from any cause either VESSEL FAILS TO UNDERSTAND THE INTENTIONS OR ACTIONS of the other, OR IS IN DOUBT WHETHER SUFFICIENT ACTION IS BEING TAKEN by the other TO AVOID COLLISION, the vessel in doubt shall

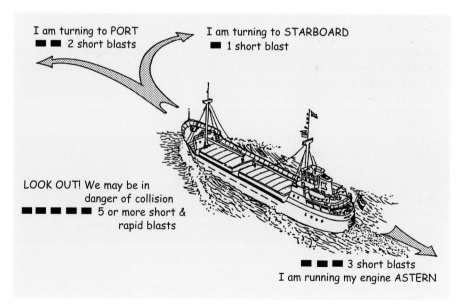

I am turning to PORT
■ ■ 2 short blasts

I am turning to STARBOARD
■ 1 short blast

LOOK OUT! We may be in danger of collision
■ ■ ■ ■ ■ 5 or more short & rapid blasts

■ ■ ■ 3 short blasts
I am running my engine ASTERN

'I can't find what "continuous short blasts" means in the almanac.'

immediately indicate such doubt by giving at least FIVE SHORT AND RAPID BLASTS on the whistle. Such signal may be supplemented by a light signal of at least five short and rapid flashes.

e) A VESSEL NEARING A BEND or an area of a channel or fairway where other vessels may be obscured by an intervening obstruction shall sound ONE PRO-LONGED BLAST. Such signal shall be ANSWERED WITH A PROLONGED BLAST by any approaching vessel that may be within hearing around the bend or behind the intervening obstruction.

Rule 35 – Sound signals in restricted visibility

In or near an area of restricted visibility, whether by day or night:

a) A POWER-DRIVEN VESSEL MAKING WAY THROUGH THE WATER shall sound, at intervals of not more than 2 minutes, ONE PROLONGED BLAST.

b) A POWER-DRIVEN VESSEL UNDER WAY BUT STOPPED and making no way through the water shall sound, at intervals of not more than 2 minutes, TWO PROLONGED BLASTS in succession with an interval of about 2 seconds between them.

Occulting light (Oc) – light periods exceed dark

c) A vessel NOT UNDER COMMAND, a vessel RESTRICTED IN HER ABILITY TO MANOEUVRE, a vessel CONSTRAINED BY HER DRAUGHT, *a SAILING vessel*, a vessel ENGAGED IN FISHING and a vessel ENGAGED IN TOWING OR PUSHING another vessel shall, instead of the signals prescribed in paragraphs a) or b) of this rule, sound at intervals of not more than 2 minutes, three blasts in succession, namely ONE PROLONGED FOLLOWED BY TWO SHORT BLASTS.

d) A vessel engaged in fishing when at anchor, and a vessel restricted in her ability to manoeuvre when carrying out her work, shall instead of the signals prescribed in paragraph g) of this rule, sound the signal prescribed in paragraph c) of this rule.

e) A VESSEL TOWED or if more than one vessel is towed the last vessel of the tow, if manned, shall at intervals of not more than 2 minutes sound four blasts in succession, namely ONE PROLONGED FOLLOWED BY THREE SHORT BLASTS.

f) [pushing tug and pushed vessel if rigidly connected are regarded as single power-driven vessel]

g) A VESSEL AT ANCHOR shall AT INTERVALS OF NOT MORE THAN ONE MINUTE RING THE BELL RAPIDLY for about 5 seconds. In a VESSEL OF 100 METRES OR MORE in length the BELL SHALL BE SOUNDED IN THE FORE PART of the vessel AND IMMEDIATELY AFTER the ringing of the bell the GONG shall be SOUNDED RAPIDLY for about 5 seconds IN THE AFTER PART of the vessel. A vessel at anchor MAY IN ADDITION sound three blasts in succession, namely ONE SHORT, ONE PROLONGED AND ONE SHORT BLAST, to give warning of her position and of the possibility of collision to an approaching vessel.

h) A VESSEL AGROUND shall give the bell signal and if required the gong signal prescribed, and IN ADDITION, give THREE SEPARATE AND DISTINCT STROKES ON THE BELL IMMEDIATELY BEFORE AND AFTER THE RAPID RINGING of the bell. A vessel aground may in addition sound an appropriate whistle signal.

i) *A VESSEL OF LESS THAN 12 METRES in length shall NOT be OBLIGED TO GIVE the ABOVE-MENTIONED SIGNALS but if she does not, shall make some other efficient sound signal at intervals of not more than 2 minutes.*

j) A PILOT VESSEL when engaged on pilotage duty MAY IN ADDITION to the signals prescribed in this rule sound AN IDENTITY SIGNAL OF FOUR SHORT BLASTS.

Anchoring

A cruising yacht should carry two anchors: a main bower and a smaller kedge, which is easier to handle and lay out from a dinghy.

There are five main anchor designs, each with their pros and cons:

- **Fisherman** – the oldest form, dismantles to stow flat, provides relatively poor holding except in weed or rocks, when it may hold better than the others.
- **Danforth** – its main advantage is the flat stowage.
- **Plough** or **CQR** – relatively good holding for a given weight, especially in mud or sand, but awkward to stow.
- **Delta** – a plough variant designed for self-launching and retrieval.
- **Bruce** – developed for oil rigs, good holding in soft ground, awkward to stow but no moving parts to crush fingers.

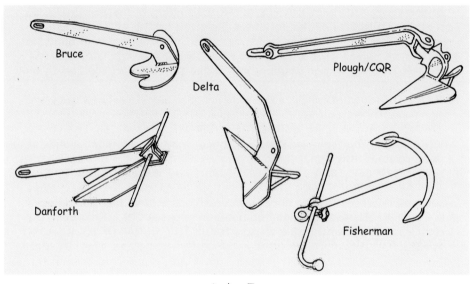

Anchor Types

Special mark

When **choosing an anchorage**, first check the nature of the seabed (Mud? Sand? Weed? Flat or steeply shelving?) then calculate the depth of water that will be left at low tide (the Rule of Twelfths). Make sure you have room to swing when the tide changes.

As a rough rule, if your anchor is attached to **chain, let out at least four times the depth**. The weight of the chain helps stabilise the boat and ensures that the pull on the anchor is horizontal, to dig it in. Flake some chain out on deck before you let go, and it helps to have a few depths marked on the chain eg with paint.

With **warp** (preferably plaited nylon) use **at least six times the depth**, but you should in any case have a few metres of chain next to the anchor, to provide some weight and prevent chafe. If in doubt, let out a bit more, and if you are still worried, don't hesitate to up anchor and try again.

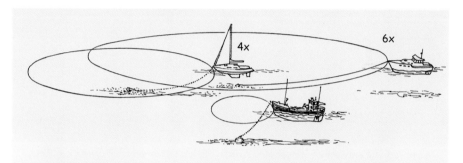

An anchorage showing the 'sailing circles' of: a yacht on 4x chain, a motor cruiser on 6x warp and a fishing boat on a fixed mooring.

Boats anchored with warp tend to 'sail' around, so beware of that when you choose your own spot. Those on shorter fixed moorings will move less, but watch that the mooring's ground chain does not foul your anchor. A buoyed 'tripping' line is one answer, to yank the anchor out the way it went in, although it is often more trouble than it is worth.

Before finally dropping the hook, visualise the anchorage when the tide turns and in the worst conditions you are likely to encounter before you leave. Would you have room to sail the anchor out at low water in a freshening onshore wind?

'We're not the only ones with problems. That big ketch behind is dragging, and fast.'

Communications

Maritime communications have evolved over hundreds of years, from the signal flags to which Nelson turned a blind eye, through semaphore, Morse telegraphy and the Aldis lamp, to various forms of voice radio. Current systems make extensive use of GPS satellites and – mostly importantly for yachtsmen – VHF (Very High Frequency) radiotelephones.

But elements of the older systems remain, and are still useful in certain situations. For example, the Morse code SOS (...---...) is still a universally recognised signal of distress; and the custom of flying a national courtesy flag at the crosstrees when visiting a foreign port is still much appreciated.

Even today, therefore, it is useful to understand the principles of signalling by flags and the old Morse code. Would-be Yachtmasters Offshore are in any case required to hold a radio operator's certificate before taking the practical exam.

Tidal stream

Flags and Morse code

Each of the **international code flags** represents a letter of the alphabet and has a 'single flag meaning'. For instance the blue and white flag for the letter 'P' – the 'Blue Peter' – is traditionally flown by a vessel about to set sail (it may also be familiar from racing start lines). On returning from a foreign port outside the EC you must fly the plain yellow 'Q' flag to tell Customs that: 'My vessel is healthy and I require free pratique'. A red flag 'B' might indicate that a tanker was discharging oil. Flag 'W' means 'I require medical assistance'.

The **ensign** is a maritime version of the national flag, flown at the stern. British yachts, like merchant vessels, fly the red ensign. Naval warships and members of the Royal Yacht Squadron fly the white ensign and some other yacht clubs have an ensign warrant entitling them to fly a blue ensign (normally used by government vessels).

'He's flying "K" Sir – I wish to communicate with you.'

When passing a warship of any nationality it is customary to 'dip' your ensign – but use this gesture sparingly unless you are prepared to be snubbed! By contrast, the custom of flying the ensign of another country at the starboard crosstrees when entering a foreign port, as a courtesy, is well observed.

The dot-dash **Morse code** survives in signals such as SOS (...---...) and V (...-) for victory and Beethoven's fifth symphony, or in a maritime context, 'I require assistance'. The telegraph buzzer and flashing aldis lamp that used this code have gone, but note that the vitally important single blast of a ship's whistle, which tells other vessels that 'I am directing my course to starboard' has a Morse equivalent in the single flash of the letter 'E'; two flashes, for 'I', means 'I am directing my course to port'.

VHF radio

The point about **VHF (Very High Frequency)**, as opposed to MF (Medium Frequency), radio is that it is virtually limited to 'line-of-sight' ranges – say about 10 miles from one yacht to another, or perhaps 30–40 miles when talking to a coastal radio station like the Coastguard. This limitation gives the paradoxical advantage that a lot of scattered craft can use the same frequency without getting in one another's way. Once in contact, VHF reception is likely to be clear; the equipment is relatively cheap; and the drain on your batteries is small. Indeed, modern technology enables yachtsmen to use a waterproof **handheld VHF** set with its own batteries and aerial – like a mobile phone – provided they accept a much shorter range of operation than the conventional set with more power and a mast-mounted aerial.

Radio channels

A band of VHF frequencies is allocated under an international agreement for use by ships and yachts, divided into a large number of 'channels', or specific frequencies. Each channel is in turn allocated to a specific function – distress calls, intership calls, port operations, and so on.

For example, **Channel 16** is both the VHF international distress frequency and the calling channel on which most other calls are briefly initiated, before switching to a working channel so as to leave it clear for other traffic. Channel 16 is therefore essential on any maritime set, as is Channel 6, the main intership working channel. The Coastguard use Channel 67, among others (see distress procedures), for communicating with small craft. Marinas in the UK often use Channel 80.

If the initial call is on Channel 16, then whoever answers will usually tell the caller to switch immediately to a specified working channel. In any event, **the maximum length of a non-distress call on Channel 16 is one minute**.

Using the same aerial to transmit and receive means that you cannot speak and listen at the same time. In other words, basic sets are limited to 'simplex' operation, in which each transmission ends with the characteristic word 'over' to invite the other person to speak (although some sets are designed for 'duplex' conversation on working channels intended for this purpose).

South cardinal buoy

Basic procedures in radio communication

All radio operators develop their own jargon and procedures in order to speed up communication and avoid any possible ambiguities. The marine fraternity are no exception; and although it may sound rather artificial at first – spelling with the phonetic alphabet, repeating key words with the introductory phrase 'I say again', turning 'a hundred and fifty' into 'one, five, zero', and so on – it has evolved from long practical experience.

The **basic procedure** is first to listen (to make sure you are not interrupting another call – especially a distress call), then identify the station or vessel you are calling, followed by your own identification, repeated, before inviting a reply: eg 'THAMES COASTGUARD – THIS IS YACHT SO AND SO, YACHT SO AND SO – OVER', to which the answer might be: 'Yacht SO AND SO – THIS IS THAMES COASTGUARD – CHANNEL 67 – OVER'.

The full procedure can be found in the RYA pamphlet G22, to which your instructor will no doubt refer you – especially if you are going on to take the practical Yachtmaster exam, for which, as we have already said, a radio operator's certificate is a prior requirement. But the main principles – such as not blocking Channel 16, keeping messages brief, formal and clear, and allowing a coastal radio station to control vital communications because of its longer effective range – are common sense.

The Phonetic Alphabet

A – Alpha	B – Bravo	C – Charlie
D – Delta	E – Echo	F – Foxtrot
G – Golf	H – Hotel	I – India
J – Juliet	K – Kilo	L – Lima
M – Mike	N – November	O – Oscar
P – Papa	Q – Quebec	R – Romeo
S – Sierra	T – Tango	U – Uniform
V – Victor	W – Whiskey	X – X-ray
Y – Yankee	Z – Zulu	

Flag W   ● ▬ ▬

Distress signals

This is another area where electronic technology and automated procedures are gradually taking over, but have not yet replaced traditional methods.

A **VHF radio distress or 'Mayday' call** (from the French *m'aidez*) should only be made when you or your yacht are in 'grave and imminent danger' and require 'immediate assistance'. The standard procedure is as follows:

Select Channel 16 at high power and speaking slowly and clearly, transmit:

- 'MAYDAY, MAYDAY, MAYDAY'
- 'THIS IS (name of yacht, repeated three times)'
- 'MAYDAY (name of yacht, spoken once)'
- 'MY POSITION IS (lat and long, or true bearing and distance from charted mark)'
- 'I AM (sinking, on fire, or whatever)'
- 'I HAVE (number of persons on board who are eg taking to a life-raft and/or firing distress rockets)'
- 'I REQUIRE IMMEDIATE ASSISTANCE'
- 'OVER'

Transmitting signals automatically

Since the introduction of the **Global Maritime Distress and Safety System (GMDSS)**, you can transmit the first part of this call (that is, the Mayday, the yacht's identity, and position) automatically, using a digital attachment to your VHF set. The attachment is known as a **Digital Selective Calling (DSC)** controller, which operates on Channel 70.

Each controller is programmed with a unique nine-digit number – the **Maritime Mobile Service Identity (MMSI) number** – which acts rather like a telephone number, rather than a name, to identify the vessel that carries it. A Coastguard station receiving an automatic distress call therefore knows who is in trouble, and if the DSC controller is linked to a GPS unit – as the GMDSS assumes – the station also receives that vessel's position (alternatively, the controller can be manually programmed with the latest position and its time). The person needing assistance waits 15 seconds for an automatic acknowledgment from the Coastguard, or a DSC-equipped ship, before repeating the distress call by voice on Channel 16, giving his or her MMSI number as well as the vessel's name or callsign.

I require medical assistance

The type of controller designed for small craft cannot automatically acknowledge a DSC distress call it receives, so it is more than usually important for a yacht in this situation to wait a while before intervening. It is vital that the rescue services, with their powerful communications, should take control as soon as possible. However, when it is clear that a distress call in any form has not been heard elsewhere, the message should be **'relayed'** (that is, passed on) on Channel 16, preceded by the words 'MAYDAY RELAY, MAYDAY RELAY, MAYDAY RELAY'.

For the foreseeable future, GMDSS will only be compulsory for merchant ships of more than 300 gross tonnes. Yachts can continue using the basic VHF system, but are warned that the Coastguard no longer maintains a dedicated 'headset' distress watch on Channel 16 (although stations still monitor this channel on a loudspeaker in operations rooms).

Another type of automatic distress signal under the GMDSS umbrella is provided by an **Emergency Position Indicating Radio Beacon (EPIRB)**; this uses satellites to alert the rescue services.

However, there are many situations falling short of 'grave and imminent danger' when help is nevertheless urgently needed, or nearby shipping needs to be informed. A yacht might be dismasted and struggling to sort out the damage, or drifting across a shipping lane with a fouled propeller. Or there might be a serious medical emergency on board. In such cases, an **'urgency' radio signal** to 'ALL STATIONS' should be made, preceded by the words 'PAN-PAN, PAN-PAN, PAN-PAN', giving the yacht's name and position, followed by a brief explanation of the problem. A call specifically seeking medical advice may be preceded by the words 'PAN-PAN MEDICO', repeated three times.

Other ways of calling for assistance

If GMDSS is at one end of the spectrum of internationally recognised distress signals, then 'flames on the vessel' is probably at the other. The means usually suggested for making this ancient signal is a burning tar barrel – something few of today's yachts carry! However, there are many **other ways of calling for assistance**:

- Red hand flare or rocket
- Orange smoke flare
- SOS Morse signal by any means
- International code letter V, by Morse or flag – 'I require assistance'
- International code flags NC
- Square flag with a ball over or under it
- Continuous sounding of a fog horn
- Continuous raising and lowering of the arms

$\longrightarrow$

Maritime and Coastguard Agency (MCA)

If you ever have to use the distress signals, it will probably be the Coastguard that sends a lifeboat or a helicopter to your rescue. The service was founded in 1822 to prevent smuggling, but nowadays it operates through a network of coastal **maritime rescue co-ordination centres**. With their powerful VHF and MF (150-mile range) radio communications, these centres are supposed to be at the heart of the GMDSS. Other responsibilities, such as a four-hourly schedule of coastal weather forecasts, have also been taken aboard. However in 2011 the Department for Transport announced a drastic reorganisation, involving a number of station closures, to take effect over the next four years. The detailed scope of the service is therefore changing throughout that period.

The MCA has adopted the relevant international safety standards established by the Safety of Life at Sea (**SOLAS**) convention, which has recently been extended to cover recreational craft. For instance it requires all vessels to carry a suitable radar reflector (more information from the RYA website www.rya.org.uk).

Safety equipment

There is no absolute safety at sea, any more than on land, so any discussion of safety equipment and practice is a matter of personal judgement and compromise. But for exam purposes, err on the side of caution and whatever guidance your instructor offers. The standards listed below are based on RYA/DfT recommendations.

On one point there can be no argument: everyone on board should have some sort of **lifejacket**. A proper lifejacket, as opposed to a **buoyancy aid**, is designed to turn an unconscious person on to his back and support his head above water. However, the advantage of some buoyancy aids – those that double as oilskins or windproof waistcoats, for example – is that you are more likely to be wearing them when you fall overboard.

The old sailor's rule about 'one hand for the ship, the other for yourself' makes perfect sense on a small yacht. Even better is a **safety harness** running on a jackstay along the deck. You will need enough harnesses to equip the watch on deck in bad weather and at night. Small children need them anyway and the DfT recommends one for every person on board. When attaching a lifeline to the boat, beware the size of U bolt that will prise the spring hook open – or use a locking hook. The lifeline should be detachable from the harness.

A yacht should carry at least two **lifebuoys** for throwing to a man overboard (buoyant kapok-filled cushions also throw well) with a long floating line available if it is appropriate. At night, an **automatic light** attached to the lifebuoy

LIFE SAVING SIGNALS

To be used by Ships, Aircraft or Persons in Distress, when communicating with life-saving stations, maritime rescue units and aircraft engaged in search and rescue operations (see also pages 109–111).

Search and Rescue Unit Replies
You have been seen, assistance will be given as soon as possible.

Maritime and Coastguard Agency

OR

Orange smoke flare.

Three white star signals or three light and sound rockets fired at approximately 1 minute intervals.

Note: Use International Code of Signals by means of lights or flags or by laying out the symbol on the deck or ground with items which have a high contrast to the background.

Surface to Air Signals

Message	ICAO/IMO Visual Signals
Require assistance	V
Require medical assistance	X
No or negative	N
Yes or affirmative	Y
Proceeding in this direction	↑

Air to Surface Direction Signals
Sequence of 3 manoeuvres meaning proceed to this direction.

1

2

3

Circle vessel at least once.

Cross low, ahead of vessel rocking wings.

Overfly vessel and head in required direction.

Note: As a non preferred alternative to rocking wings, varying engine tone or volume may be used.

Your assistance is no longer required

Cross low, astern of vessel rocking wings.

Shore to Ship Signals
Safe to land here.

Vertical waving of both arms, white flag, light or flare.

— K

Morse code signal by light or sound

OR

Landing here is dangerous. Additional signals mean safer landing in direction indicated.

Horizontal waving of white flag, light or flare. Putting one flag, light or flare on ground and moving off with a second indicates direction of safer landing.

S: • • •
R: • — •

Morse code signals by light or sound.

R: Land to the right of your current heading.
L: Land to the left of your current heading.

OR

Air to Surface Replies
Message Understood.

Drop a message

OR

Rocking wings.

(green)

OR

(red)

Flashing landing or navigation lights on and off twice.

— T   OR   • — •
                    R

Morse code signal by light.

Message Not Understood – Repeat.

Straight and level flight

OR

Circling.

• — •   OR   • — — •   —
    R   P   T

Morse code signal by light.

Surface to Air Replies
Message Understood – I will comply.

Change course to required direction.

OR

— T

Morse code signal by light.

I am unable to comply.

Note: Use the signal most appropriate to prevailing conditions.

— •
N

OR

Morse code signal by light.

(red/white)

Code & answering pendant 'Close Up'.

OR

(blue/white)

International Flag 'N'.

(the light comes on when it inverts in a floating position) could be a lifesaver. Even during the day, keeping a continuous watch on the man overboard is one of the most vital aspects of the drill – and made much easier if you can drop a tall **danbuoy** of the type that fishermen use to mark lobster pots.

Man overboard

There is no single 'best method' for recovering a man overboard. So much depends on circumstances and how actively the person in the water can help himself. So be guided by your instructor. But for an auxiliary powered yacht there are perhaps two main techniques, both preceded, if possible, by throwing a lifebuoy (have one mounted in the cockpit and the other on the foredeck).

Under sail, turn immediately on to a reach (taking care not to lose sight of the missing crew member), go about, reach back and round up close to windward of the casualty. It will probably pay to let the headsail fly, or maybe furl it altogether, and control your speed by playing the mainsheet.

If an engine is instantly available, the alternative is to get rid of the headsail, circle the man overboard under power and approach upwind with the mainsail freed and flapping. In this case watch for trailing lines round the prop. But of course you will have to react to actual circumstances. The best answer may be an immediate 'crash stop', perhaps heaving-to.

'We were thinking of having a person-overboard drill, Joan.'

When getting someone back on board – possibly injured, cold or exhausted – the first move should be to get them attached to the boat. Lifting a more or less helpless person is surprisingly difficult and will probably be much easier with a **deep boarding ladder**.

Abandoning ship

If you ever have to put out a Mayday call and abandon ship, you may be relying on the rescue services ashore in the form of a lifeboat or helicopter – when your job is to co-operate efficiently – or taking to your own dinghy or liferaft.

Few yachts nowadays tow a rigid tender and only large vessels can conveniently carry one on deck. A suitably sized **inflatable dinghy** with bailer attached is in any case likely to be a better bet – but only if it is already inflated, or the situation allows time for the lengthy, awkward procedure of inflation (some yachtsmen compromise by carrying it half-inflated).

The alternative is a **liferaft**, thrown into the sea and inflated by jerking an attached line. Liferafts come in various sizes, designed and equipped for different circumstances. If stowed on deck they should be secured with the simplest possible lashing, held together with a single knot. Their use should be absolutely the last resort, if the yacht is obviously sinking fast or on fire. Crews have been lost by prematurely taking to a liferaft – for one thing it is more difficult to spot from the air.

Your chances of surviving this sort of emergency will probably be increased if you keep a **grab bag** handy in the cockpit, packed or available for things you might need – flares, torch, handheld VHF, knife, mobile phone, first aid including seasickness pills, and water.

If a **helicopter** comes to your rescue, you may paradoxically be instructed to go overboard deliberately – in a dinghy or liferaft at the end of a long warp, or just in a lifejacket – so as to make winching you up easier. The winching wire will be preceded by a light line to guide it down (let the wire touch the water before handling it, to discharge static electricity).

If a winchman comes down to take charge of the lift, he will probably land on the port quarter, so if you have a mainsail set, maintain course on the port tack. Clear the decks of anything that might snag the wire – *and never make it fast*. The lifting strop goes under your armpits, and tightens with a toggle; keep your arms down, even though this feels unnatural. If radio communication is possible (once overhead, the noise of the helicopter will swamp the VHF), it will almost certainly be on Channel 16.

Distress flares

These come in various forms – orange smoke (visible on a clear day up to about 3 miles); red hand flares (visible up to about 10 miles at night in clear visibility); red parachute rockets (visible at more than 20 miles unless fired into low cloud). The minimum recommended pack depends on the cruising range:

- **Inshore** (sheltered waters such as an estuary) – **2 hand flares, 2 orange smokes.**
- **Coastal** (up to 10 miles from land) – **2 parachute rockets, 2 hand flares, 2 orange smokes**.
- **Offshore** (more than 10 miles from land) – **4 parachute rockets, 4 hand flares, 2 buoyant orange smokes**.

Many skippers also like to carry **white hand flares** as a 'deterrent' to ships on a collision course at night. A few yachts carry a Very pistol which fires small flares.

As a last resort, a **powerful waterproof torch** is obviously better than nothing. In fact it is good practice to have two torches – one for everyday use, the other handy for real emergencies.

Fire and explosions on board

Fire can be more dangerous at sea than on land, even though one is surrounded by water. Any yacht with either an engine – especially a petrol engine – or cooking equipment needs at least one fire extinguisher. The recommended equipment for smaller yachts is two 1.5-kilogram dry powder **extinguishers** (carbon dioxide or foam are alternatives, but powder is what the fire brigade use for their own vehicles). They should be stored away from potential sources of fire, one at each end of the boat. Large motor yachts should have an automatic extinguisher built into the engine compartment.

A **fire blanket** is worth having to smother fires, for example in the galley. And of course sea water may be the answer, provided you are not dealing with spilt engine fuel. In any case, every boat needs at least one **bucket** on a lanyard, preferably two, and a flat bailer for the dinghy.

Far worse than a simple fire is the danger of exploding petrol fumes or cooking gas. This gas is heavier than air, so if it does escape it tends to collect in the bilges – which is why gas bottles should be stored in a separate locker that drains overboard. The most important single precaution is always to close the valve on the bottle when it is not needed. If there is a leak, a **gas detector** will provide warning. A diaphragm pump will help to clear the bilges.

Radio/TV mast

Two **pumps**, which are easy to dismantle and can be worked from secure positions, are basic safety equipment. If possible make one of them an electric pump, which keeps going when you and your crew tire.

First aid kit

The boat's **first aid kit** should include seasickness tablets, dressings for burns, and painkillers. But perhaps the most important item is a book of first aid instructions, including mouth-to-mouth resuscitation and ways of treating hypothermia – because not knowing what to do for the best is sometimes the most frightening thing about an accident or injury. *Reeds Nautical Almanac* has a useful first aid section. In any case, a first aid certificate is a prior requirement of the practical Yachtmaster exam.

Safety equipment checklist

- Lifejackets – one for each crew member
- Safety harnesses – one for each crew member
- Lifebuoys – two
- Danbuoy
- Buoyant automatic light
- Boarding ladder
- Liferaft – inflated inflatable, or rigid dinghy
- Flares – four red rockets, four red hand flares, two orange smokes, two white flares
- Two 1.5-kilogram fire extinguishers
- First aid kit
- Fire blanket
- Waterproof torch
- Radar reflector
- Foghorn
- Bilge pumps – two
- Bucket

Radar reflectors and mobile phones

One piece of safety equipment that has become increasingly valuable as merchant ships get bigger and faster, and perhaps more careless of their small sisters, is a **radar reflector**, hoisted as high as possible. The basic type consists of aluminium plates slotted together in a shape known as an octahedral, and fixed so that it presents one of its hollow reflective corners to the radar transmitter's beam (and 'catches water' in the upper corner). Possibly more efficient (that is, producing a bigger blip on the radar screen) are the kind of reflectors that encapsulate a number of hollow metal shapes in a plastic casing, which then hoists naturally in the correct position.

In its early forms, the **mobile phone** was sometimes scorned by mariners because it is evidently not a substitute for a VHF radio. Yet within its limited range it can be immensely valuable aboard a boat – increasingly so if it is internet-capable.

Stability and buoyancy of yachts

Newly marketed yachts must nowadays demonstrate that they have the stability and buoyancy appropriate to their design category – 'A' (Ocean), 'B' (Offshore), 'C' (Inshore), or 'D' (Sheltered Waters). Conscious of this, the RYA publishes a booklet G23, analysing the factors that affect these qualities. Apart from the special case of the catamaran, the main point to note is that adding equipment aloft – particularly mast-mounted radar antennas and headsail furling gear – will reduce stability. Commonsense it may be, but this is a point still sometimes ignored.

Coping with bad weather

The most obvious kind of bad weather is a gale, but in a shipping lane like the Dover Strait, half choked with sandbanks and a ship passing every five minutes, **fog** can be just as much of a hazard – especially since sea fog can coexist with a fresh breeze that in itself brings problems for small sailing craft. At least the wind brings manoeuvrability, removing that sense of helplessness that comes with lying becalmed in poor visibility. If there are ships about in these conditions, it is a fine point of judgement as to when to switch on an auxiliary engine – thereby exchanging the ability to hear danger approaching, for the speed to get out of the way if it actually arrives. Stopping the engine periodically to listen is probably the best tactic. In any case, the engine should be warmed up and ready for instant use.

Commonsense precautions in fog include plotting the most accurate possible position before it clamps down (this is when the methodical navigator scores), wearing lifejackets, having a dinghy towing or ready to launch, and

Occluded front

using a foghorn (though on a big ship's bridge it will not be heard in time to make any difference). In many situations, much the safest course will be to sound your way into shallow water where large vessels cannot follow, or at least keep clear of obvious shipping lanes.

Fog precautions

- Plot position at first sign of worsening visibility
- Maintain plot, eg with GPS
- Hoist radar reflector if not permanently rigged
- Put on lifejackets
- Launch (or at least prepare) dinghy
- Increase look-out; if under power stop engine often to listen
- Sound foghorn every two minutes
- Consider sounding into shallow water

The key to **surviving strong winds** in relative comfort and safety is anticipation, starting with your honed weather forecasting skills and a basic decision as to whether to run for shelter or find some sea room to ride it out – a choice that even lifeboatmen have sometimes got wrong.

In rough weather almost everything is much more difficult and tiring than usual, even just moving about or filling a kettle, and seasickness may make matters even worse. The aim, therefore, is to reduce to a minimum the number of things that will have to be done during a blow by thinking ahead and making preparations – putting on oilskins before you get wet; taking the seasickness tablets early; stowing loose gear securely; sealing hatches; getting out the lifejackets and safety harnesses; shortening sail early (before you really need to, unless of course you are racing); preparing some simple food; looking up navigational data you may need; planning where you will bolt if an unexpected gear failure forces you to run off downwind, and so on. If night is coming on, all this still applies only *more* so.

When heavy weather cannot be avoided, the way to make it relatively comfortable is to pull down one more reef than you think you absolutely need. And if there's a job to be done on deck, don't forget the ancient tactic of 'heaving-to' (jib aback, mainsail close hauled and helm lashed down); it really does transform the situation.

Heavy weather checklist

- Secure loose gear on deck and below.
- Put on lifejackets and safety harnesses.
- Take seasickness tablets if required.
- Take in reef or reefs (maybe one more than immediately required).
- Rig jackstays if not permanent.
- Prepare simple food in accessible locker.
- Pre-plan navigation and escape routes.

Environmental awareness

People are becoming more and more concerned about protecting the environment, and this extends to the sea – and hence to yachtsmen. Four **basic principles** are endorsed by the RYA:

- **Garbage** – do not dump it at sea, but keep it to dispose of ashore.
- **Oily wastes** – prevent any discharge of oil, fuel or similar harmful substances at sea.
- **Sewage** – do not discharge a sea toilet close inshore.
- **Toxic wastes** – keep toxic or damaging chemicals (such as anti-fouling) out of the sea.

Well, that's it! We hope we have done our bit to help you with your Yachtmaster course. Good luck with those exams, and good sailing!

Dries 2.7 metres above LW

Index